TUNISIA

STABILITY AND GROWTH IN THE NEW MILLENNIUM

TUNISIA

STABILITY AND GROWTH IN THE NEW MILLENNIUM

Jon Marks and Mark Ford

Published by Euromoney Books

in association with

Comete Engineering S.A.

Financière Tunisienne S.A.

Groupe Carte

Published by
Euromoney Books
Nestor House, Playhouse Yard
London EC4V 5EX
Tel: +44 (0)20 7779 8860 Fax: +44 (0)20 7779 8541
E-mail: books@euromoneyplc.com
Website: www.euromoneybooks.com

ISBN 1 85564 902 0

Typeset by Julie Foster and Euromoney Books
Printed in England by Clifford Press, Coventry

TUNISIA
N
Capital
Major Town
Major Town & Port
Town
Port
International Airport
Lake
Seasonal lake
Primary road
Secondary road
International border
District border
Rail
0 50 100
Kilometres
Gulf of Tunis
Cap Bon
Bizerte
Menzel-Bourguiba
Bizerte
Mateur
La Goulette
Nabeul
Kerkouane
Menzel-Temime
Korbous
Tabarka
Carthage
Radès
Ariana
Tunis
Béja
Bousalem
Medjez
Ben Arous
Majardah
Jundubah
Béja
Nabeul
Hammamet
Ghardimaou
Medjerda Valley
El Fahs
Zagouan
Zaghouan
Gulf of Hammamet
Enfidah
El Kef
Siliana
Sousse
Port el Kantaoui
El Kef
Sousse
Monastir
Moknine
Maktar
M'Saken
Kalaat-Khasba
Monastir
Mahdia
Karouan
Ksour Essaf
Kairouan
El Jem
Kasserine
Mahdia
Sheitla
Kasserine
Sfax
Sidi Bouzid
Sfax
Kerkennah
Feriana
Mediterranean Sea
Gafsa
Meknassy
Gafsa
Gulf of Gabès
Mides
La Skhira
El Guettar
Redeyef
Metlaoui
Chebika
Tozeur
Houmt-Souk
Djerba
Gabès
Jerba
Ajim
Nefta
Tozeur
Gabès
Jorf
Zarzis
Chott el Jerid
Kebili
Matmata
Medenine
Douz
El Faouar
Ben Guardane
Medenine
Ghomrassen
Chenini
Kebili
Remada
LIBYA
Tataouine
Borj
ALGERIA
Sahara Desert
Atlantic Ocean
France
Italy
Spain
Turkey
Tunisia
Morocco
Algeria
Libya
Egypt

The authors

Jon Marks is a British expert on North Africa and the Middle East, writing for a range of publications on Maghreb business, policy and history since 1984.

Mark Ford is a business development specialist and writer on a range of economic issues. He is a director of Cross-border Information Ltd.

Acknowledgements

The authors would like to thank Industry Minister Moncef Ben Abdallah, former Banque Centrale de Tunisie Governor Mohamed Beji Hamda, Housing and Equipment Minister Slaheddine Belaïd, Communications Minister Ahmed Friaa, Office National de la Famille et de la Population Director Nabiha Gueddana, International Co-operation and Foreign Investment Minister Fethi Merdassi, National Economy Minister Abdellatif Saddem, their officials and other Tunisian and international experts who all gave up their time to be interviewed in connection with this book.

The authors would like to thank Euromoney Books for their efficient handling of the text, for which they were ultimately responsible.

Euromoney Books would like to thank Lilia Abdelwahed of Cofib Capital Finances and Richard Banks of LCI Ltd.

All the pictures in the book except the co-publishers' were supplied by Capstone Design.

Door at Sidi-bou-Said

Contents

1 *Introduction: creating a new Mediterranean economy*

Look deeply into Tunisia's history and a number of themes echo through the ages. This corner of the southern Mediterranean has tempted generations of invaders, most of whom have left their mark on at least the coastal fringes of what is now Tunisia. The land has long been settled by sophisticated urban cultures – from the Phoenicians establishing a settlement at Carthage to the early Roman Christians, several Arab dynasties and the Ottomans. These have found Tunisia to be a hospitable place from which to develop their trade routes and diplomatic relations. In what can be a tough neighbourhood, Tunisia is known for its douceur de vivre (sweet living) – a factor in today's tourism boom and a significant selling point when selling the economy as a suitable place to base investments in the Mediterranean basin region.

While so many of North Africa's colonial-era heroes were warriors – such as Emir Abdelkrim in Morocco's Rif, Algeria's Emir Abdelkader and Libya's Omar Al Mokhtar – the figure who marked Tunisia in the 19th century was an Ottoman general, Kherredine Pasha. His reputation was based on a talent for administration, rather than warfare, fitting into a tradition that remains to this day. Visit government offices in modern Tunis, and long traditions of civil service persist. This taste for administration has a plus side – Tunisia is by all accounts more efficiently managed than any of its neighbours. According to Economic Development Minister Abdellatif Saddem:

> Ideas now being put into practise, such as allowing citizens to submit their tax statements from a distance, show how we are removing the citizen from direct state control. We do this coming from a tradition where Tunisia has a clean, non-corrupt administration. We are proud of our Transparency International rating.

The downside of this administrative tradition is that the state has come to play a leading role in economic management. After Independence the government's focus was on state-led economic development, including the collectivisation of agriculture and government control of major industrial enterprises. This was not popular, and by 1969, popular resistance to these moves and economic stagnation had convinced independent Tunisia's founding President Habib Bourguiba of the need for a relatively free market economy. Thus the Tunisian private sector was never crushed during the 1960s and 1970s – when a taste for state socialism and collectivist policies swept North Africa, as with much of the developing, post-colonial world.

Zitouna Great Mosque

Government Place, Tunis

Even so, in Bourguiba's mixed economy, the state played a predominant role in economic management and one of President Zine El Abidine Ben Ali's preoccupations since replacing the ailing Bourguiba on 7 November 1987 has been to roll back the state's dominance of microeconomic activity.

This has been achieved to a significant extent – although not as quickly as many economic liberals would like. Tunisia's government remains committed to reform mixed with 'gradualism', but is equally determined that the pace of economic change is timed so as not to upset the country's social fabric. While this has meant that the pace of privatisation and other policies has gone more slowly than in some other countries, officials point to the soundness of this policy with reference to Tunisia's success in avoiding social disorder.

During a period when the clash between traditional state structures and radical Islam has been so apparent in other countries, Tunisia has maintained social peace, not only through the rigorous policing encouraged by President Ben Ali but to a large extent because of a carefully managed economic transition. This means that Tunisia now has the region's largest middle class and very respectable national income, despite lacking the large-scale natural resources enjoyed by its bigger neighbours. The role of government is now to maintain this positive trend. As Economic Development Minister Saddem puts it:

> Ben Ali has been successful because he listens to Tunisian professionals and to the people; he listened to business and its complaints, [and] in 2000 decided to cut the amount of authorisations companies needed to operate. These have now been reduced to a minimum... [On the social front] the challenge is to meet the fast-rising demands of the people – who can demand a lot of government – while keeping the budget under control.

Critics argue that state intervention still goes far beyond these bounds. The legalised opposition to Ben Ali's mighty Rassemblement Constitutionnel Démocratique (RCD) party remains weak, despite efforts to bring more opposition deputies into parliament and local government. Whatever the reasons for this, it is clear that Ben Ali's formula to build a new Tunisia will continue to provide the catalyst for Tunisia's economic development, which hinges on an investment drive that, increasingly, is bringing Tunisia into the European economic space. This is a space it has occupied at various times during its past, as when it was the granary and intellectual powerhouse of the Roman world, and later when it was colonised by a major European power, France.

A Mediterranean hub

In Ben Ali's vision of the new Tunisia, connections are everything. Road and rail links must connect Tunisia's vibrant cities and provide better access to and from less-developed interior areas. Air and sea routes must connect Tunisia with its international partners. Health, education and other social services, as well as every area of the economy and all Tunisians depend on reliable connections to sources of power and water. Connection to telephones and the information highway (discussed in Chapter 8) are vital for integrating activities throughout the country and binding Tunisia into the international community.

Such connections have always been a part of Tunisian history. The Phoenicians, the foremost traders of the classical age, developed their major settlement at Carthage, on the coast of northern Tunisia close to Tunis, in 814 BC. Underlining the area's strategic location, Carthage – site of today's presidential palace and acres of impressive classical ruins – was built to control access to Sicily. As the Phoenicians' original home base of Tyre, in what is now Lebanon, came under pressure from Assyrians and Persians, and the Ptolomeic Greeks came to dominate Egypt and Cyrenaica (in what is now Libya), Carthage became the hub for their new maritime commercial empire. This took the Phoenicians far beyond Mare Nostrum into the Atlantic – providing a point of historical reference which resonates with Tunisian policy-makers to this day.

The emergence of Rome created a new dynamic on the North African coast, and conflict with Carthage over Sicily (from which the Carthaginians were expelled in 201 BC). The conflict saw the emergence of North Africa's most famous general, Hannibal, who took his forces into northern Europe, but eventually the Roman legions won out, taking their campaign to Carthage itself, which was razed in 146 BC. The Carthaginian Empire's heartlands became the Roman province of Africa.

Roman Africa was a wealthy province, as is underlined by such remarkable ruins as the coliseum at El Djem, built to entertain a Romano-African population made rich on its cultivation of cereals, olives and other crops to feed the empire. Tunis' Bardo Museum houses a treasure of mosaics and other artefacts from this civilisation. However, it was not just in material things that Roman Tunisia was to flourish. North Africa was a breeding ground for new Christian doctrine, represented by St. Augustine, the greatest of the early Christian fathers. Christianity was further reinforced when Byzantine control was consolidated by the Emperor Justinian's forces in 533 AD – but Byzantine administration (and taxation) was not popular among the local Berber population, making it easier for the next wave of invaders to have the most profound influence on Tunisia little over a century later.

An Islamic country

A decade after the death of the Prophet Mohammed, Arab armies entered Egypt (642 AD) and then Cyrenaica. In 665, they moved again and Okba Ibn Nafaa conquered Tunisia. He established Kairouan in 670, still the holiest site in Tunisia and considered one of Islam's great religious centres. Ommayyad Kairouan provided the base from which much of the Maghreb region was converted to Islam – but early alliances with local Berber groups were not consolidated and in the next two decades warfare ensued against local leaders such as Kusayla and Al-Kahina, and the remaining Byzantine garrisons at Carthage and Bizerte. The latter fell in 690, and Tunis was founded as a counterweight to the old Phoenician capital (now a suburb of the capital). By 732, Islamic armies had conquered most of Spain and Portugal; their advance was stopped at Poitiers by Charles Martel, and the balance of power in the early Medieval Mediterranean basin was established.

Arab rulers sought to impose their rule, and most importantly their values, on North Africa's local populations. In this, introducing their religion proved even more successful than spreading their language. Often these values became far more deeply rooted than their political rule – during centuries when Arab dynasties waxed and waned – and foreign powers (such as Spain in the 16th century) were able to play a role.

Tunis was integrated into the Ottoman Empire by Sinan Pasha, and by 1591, a system of janissary[1] leadership was in place with a bey (governor of a district or province) imposed on the local pasha (Turkish officer of high rank). In the early 18th century, the Ottoman regency of Algiers tried to conquer Tunisia (then still ruled from Istanbul) and Hussein Ben Ali became bey in 1705; this started the Husseinite Dynasty that was to rule until 1957, autonomous of the Sublime Porte.

European intervention

Tunisia was ruled as a colony of France for only a relatively short period (1881–1956). Despite the efforts of enlightened administrators such as Kherredine Pasha, the maladministration of a decadent beylical regime played its part in opening the door to European conquest, as did a mounting external debt – providing a historical lesson of which Tunisian decision-makers remain well aware to this day. However well, or badly run the Regency of Tunisia proved to be, the great powers had decided it was not to remain outside their grasp, and the 1878 Congress of Berlin decided that Tunisia should fall under French influence. Earlier in the century, Tunis had enjoyed a strong British influence – reflected in the mighty British embassy building by the gates of Tunis' old city, the Medina, and in one of the most impressive ambassador's residences anywhere, situated on the Route de La Marsa. All that was needed was a pretext, and in 1881 French troops invaded on the pretext that a border tribe, the Khroumir, had been raiding into Algeria, the jewel in the French colonial crown.

Doorway, Bardo Museum, Tunis

The French Protectorate was opposed by many Tunisians, but at first violent rebellion came mainly from tribes in the south. France developed the fertile areas of the country as a European settler colony with around 100,000 people. In fact, the largest settler group were not French (as in Algeria, now part of metropolitan France) but Italian. They exploited around 800,000 hectares of the best farmland. In the cities, a French-speaking business and administrative elite dominated.

As the 20th century opened, urban opposition to colonial occupation gathered pace, led by the new generation of largely French-educated politicians (backed by the ulema[2]). This opposition was reflected in trade union activity – helping to make the Union Générale Tunisienne du Travail (UGTT) a major player in post-independence politics – and the rise of an highly articulate leader in the French-trained lawyer Habib Bourguiba, a graduate of the Lycée Carnot.

In 1934, Bourguiba took over a radicalised nationalist movement, renamed the Néo-Destour. This is the party which became the Parti Socialiste Destourien (PSD) of Bourguiba's latter years and is now Ben Ali's RCD. Before World War II, the Néo-Destour faced the panoply of French colonial repression. After the war – when Tunisia had been invaded by the Germans – attitudes began to change, ultimately making it easier for Bourguiba to mobilise his mass movement for independence. Rising nationalist pressure led by the Néo-Destour and its allies, including the UGTT, resulted in autonomy from France in 1955 and full independence on 20 March 1956.

Independence and after

Bourguiba naturally assumed the presidency, and the Néo-Destour's structures became those of the independent state. Now to be resolved were the issues of state building, economic construction and where to situate Tunisia in the world. Thorny questions were posed by the nature of Tunisia's future relationship with France, which was still at war in Algeria (some of whose Front de Libération Nationale structures and leadership Tunisia sheltered) and which maintained an important military base at Bizerte.

When in 1958 French aircraft bombed the Tunisian border village of Sakiet Sidi Youssef – still a point of reference among advocates of Maghreb unity – Bourguiba demanded that French forces should abandon the Bizerte naval base. In the stand-off that followed, around 1,000 Tunisians died before France withdrew. Meanwhile, land belonging to European settlers was expropriated and most of them moved out.

These struggles coloured Tunisia's early relations with Europe, but Bourguiba was essentially a francophile and pro-western. This filtered through into Tunisia's foreign policy meaning that as the radical 1960s and 1970s progressed, Tunisia was most usually seen as a western ally, and a useful bridge with the Arab world. This position – maintained by a president who quickly established his credentials as an elder statesman in international affairs – meant that Tunisia often punched well above its weight in international diplomacy, and was well-placed to

Colosseum, El Jem

play an important role in the great events of the day. This became especially apparent when, in 1982, Tunis took in the Palestine Liberation Organisation (PLO) leadership after it was driven from Beirut.

Bourguiba also sought to promote Tunisia's virtues as a financial centre – and in the early 1980s seemed poised to win much of the Arab banking business that had previously been transacted through Beirut. However, Tunisia's claims to become a major offshore banking centre quickly ran out of steam as domestic economic problems started to weigh heavily on the government and population. This exploded into social unrest in late 1983/early 1984.

Reform and transition

The first decades of Bourguiba's presidency established the shape of modern Tunisia – a country based on social tolerance and an enlightened attitude to the development of the family (reflected in the impressive demographic and social data examined in Chapter 2), with a strong administrative tradition and a mixed economy. In his latter years, Bourguiba (who became

Detail of the 'Triumph of Neptune' mosaic, Bardo Museum, Tunis

president-for-life in 1975) was concerned not only with challenges to his power – first from radical leftists, then from radical Islamists- but also with his eventual succession.

By 1987, Tunisia was being widely seen as a country of impending crisis rather than as a zone of stability. It was to prove a watershed year. A competent economic team was brought in and negotiated a wide-ranging economic restructuring agreement with the International Monetary Fund (IMF). This programme, including privatisation as part of a deep shift from public to private-sector management of the economy, has formed the basis for policy ever since. Then, Prime Minister Zine El Abidine Ben Ali, who since becoming Interior Minister in 1986, quickly and efficiency emerged the most likely and popular candidate to replace Bourguiba.

Bourguiba's removal reduced tensions which were threatening to come to a head. Ben Ali offered a new political liberalisation, with the development of a multi-party system and greater freedom of expression. As importantly for most Tunisians, he offered the prospect of a secure future, when the country's much-vaunted stability had before been thrown into doubt. In the hopeful period that followed his takeover, political prisoners were released, new parties were permitted and a National Pact was established to create a new social consensus. These policies have continued to this day (most successful has been achieving social consensus through negotiations between the authorities, employers and unions).

Ben Ali's legacy will be defined by efforts now under way to consolidate economic reforms and the foundation of macroeconomic stability laid down in the past decade. Signs that a more vibrant private sector, comprising local entrepreneurs and foreign investors, is breaking through to help create sustained growth – now running at 5 per cent plus annually – suggest that Tunisia can achieve its goal, of becoming a fully fledged member of the European economic space within the next decade. Efforts to build stability in North Africa through a revived Maghreb Arab Union (UMA) and, especially, closer ties to Europe through the European Association Agreement (described in following chapters) will be crucial in this respect.

From an economic standpoint, the country's model for achieving sustainable growth through a process of steady reform is delivering tangible results. Tunisia can again claim to be emerging as a trading and communications hub in the Mediterranean basin. Building on those foundations will require substantial further effort. Refreshingly, most Tunisians are aware that this is the case and are prepared to work hard to ensure that their country fulfils its historic vocation. In an Arab/African world so often wracked with doubts and undermined by conflicts Tunisia, as one slogan has it, is 'a country that works'. It is also a country with a promising future, whose advances to date are more than worth preserving for the coming generations.

---

1. Janissaries were Turkish infantry.
2. A body of Muslim scholars recognised as having specialist knowledge of Islamic sacred law and theology.

2 *Resources and infrastructure*

A strategic crossroads

Tunisia is strategically positioned at the crossroads of Africa, the Middle East and Europe. Located in North Africa but only 140 kilometres across the Strait of Sicily to Europe, it has a 16,000-kilometre Mediterranean coastline to the north and east. It shares a 965-kilometre border with Algeria in the west and a 459-kilometre border with Libya in the south-east. With a land area of 162,155 square kilometres, Tunisia is a very much smaller country than its North African neighbours, slightly larger than Greece.

The country comprises four distinct physical regions. Off the Mediterranean coastline are many small islands, notably Djerba in the south and Kerkennah in the east. Behind the coastline are pine-wooded hills, rich pastures, orchards, vineyards and olive groves.

The mountainous north has two ranges: the Northern Tell and the more southerly High Tell. Separating the two ranges is the fertile Medjerda valley, a major cereal-producing agricultural region. The area has several forested mountains higher than 1,000 metres. Mount Ash-Shaambi, near the Algerian border, is the highest point in Tunisia at 1,544 metres above sea level. Tunisia has one perennial river, the Majardah (Medjerda). It is used to generate hydroelectric power and for irrigation.

Central Tunisia is a semi-arid steppe plateau elevated about 500 metres above sea level. The low-lying Sahel, a flat westward extension of the coastal plain that extends into Libya, has seasonal salt lakes and olive groves.

In southern Tunisia lie a series of chotts (shallow salt lakes) and some spectacular date palm plantations. Rich artesian water sources make well-cultivated oases possible in the southern part of Tunisia as it gives way to the sand and rock of the Sahara desert.

The fast-growing capital city, Tunis, is situated on the north coast; it is the country's commercial and administrative centre. Midway down the east coast is the major industrial city of Sfax. Other major cities include Gabès, Sousse, Bizerte, Beja, Karouan, Gafsa and Tozeur are major inland centres in the south.

Maximising a varied resource base

Tunisia does not have an especially rich store of natural resources compared with its oil-rich neighbours, Algeria and Libya. This means that its future relies on the development and

Jebel Dahar

management of human capital, supported by sound transportation and communications infrastructures. It is the application of these resources that will determine the country's economic and social future. This chapter examines the store of human and physical capital available to Tunisia's planners, and to the investors they are keen to attract.

Exhibit 2.1
Land overview ('000 hectares)

	('000 hectares)
Cultivated land	10,300
Fertile land	2,900
Land with average to weak fertility	6,500
Uncultivated land	7,100
Sandy accumulations	3,200
Saline stretches	2,000
Rocky outcrops	1,900
Natural formations	4,000
Natural forests	368
Reforestry	287
Bushland and scrubland	275
Alfalfa layers	434
River courses	2,637

Source: Publicomm.

Natural resources and energy

Although not rich in natural resources, Tunisia does however have moderate deposits of onshore and offshore oil and gas. In terms of minerals, Tunisia has significant quantities of phosphates, as well as some iron ore, lead, zinc and salt.

Climatic and soil conditions in parts of the country are conducive to the production of dates and olives for oil. Tunisia is the world's leading date producer and the fourth largest producer of olive oil. The country also produces grapes, citrus fruit, market produce and cereals. However, fertile land is at a premium, and farming is not encouraged by sometimes adverse and unpredictable climatic conditions (see Exhibit 2.1).

Climate and geography

Climatic differences in Tunisia are marked. From north to south, the climate grows hotter and drier. The north has a typically Mediterranean climate with hot dry summers and mild rainy winters. Temperatures moderated by the sea average 7°C (45°F) in winter and 32°C (90°F) in summer.

In the arid south, summer is an uncomfortable mix of soaring temperatures and high humidity. The hot, dry, southerly Sirocco winds that blow from the Sahara adversely impact plant and animal life and frequently push temperatures up to 45°C. At the far south of Tunisia where the Sahara desert begins, days are hot and nights are cool.

Critical to Tunisia's economic performance and the distribution of its population, rainfall is irregular and droughts are common. Average annual rainfall is estimated at 207 millimetres, but almost half the country receives less than 100 millimetres a year. Only in the extreme north does rainfall reach 1,500 millimetres a year. About 80 per cent of the rain falls between October and March. Some areas are without rain for several years.

Coastal and water resources

Tunisia has moderate fish stocks off what might be considered its prime natural resource asset – a Mediterranean coastline that attracts tourists.

The country has limited water resources, unevenly distributed in geographical and seasonal terms. Population growth and socio-economic development have meant a corresponding growth in water needs. The result has been increasing pressure on the country's capacity to provide this rare resource in sufficient quantities.

The National Water Resources Development Plan – launched in 1990 and evaluated at cabinet level in early-2000 – planned to provide 1.4 billion cubic metres (bcm) of water, but has only generated 1 bcm. Irrigated areas have expanded to 345,000 hectares from 256,000

Exhibit 2.2
Water overview

Total quantity of water	5 bcm
Number of reservoirs	22 with 1.9 bcm capacity.
National Company for Water Distribution supplied:	
Consumers (1998)	1.4 million (200,000 in 1974)
Production (1998)	326 mcm (142 mcm in 1974)

Exhibit 2.3

Energy overview

Proven oil reserves (1/1/00E)	308 million barrels
Total oil production (1999E)	82,000 bbl/d (nearly all crude)
Oil consumption (1998E)	79,000 bbl/d
Net oil exports (1999E)	3,000 bbl/d
Crude refining capacity (1/1/00E)	34,000 bbl/d
Natural gas reserves (1/1/00E)	2,750 billion cubic feet (bcf)
Natural gas production (1998E)	67 bcf
Natural gas consumption (1998E)	104 bcf
Net natural gas imports (1998E)	37 bcf
Recoverable coal reserves (12/31/96)	None
Coal consumption/imports (1998E)	0.1 million short tons
Electric generation capacity (1/1/98E)	1.7 gigawatts (96% thermal, 4% hydroelectric)
Electricity generation (1998E)	7.9 billion kilowatt hours

E = Estimate.

Source: US Energy Information Administration.

hectares and drinking water is now supplied to 78 per cent of villages, compared with 33 per cent before the plan.

Energy demand

Demand for energy for commercial and industrial purposes is growing fast, at an estimated 7 per cent annually. Around 95 per cent of Tunisian homes have access to electricity, over 90 per cent of which is from oil and gas powered generators, with the rest generated by hydropower. See Exhibit 2.3 for an energy overview.

Demographic characteristics

Over the past four decades, Tunisia's demographic profile has changed significantly. More Tunisians now live in urban areas as the economic emphasis has shifted from agriculture to other forms of activity. Life expectancy has lengthened and infant mortality has reduced as a result of improved welfare and healthcare standards.

The most remarkable demographic changes have occurred within the country's social fabric. Polygamy was abolished in 1956 when the Personal Status Code was introduced to regulate marriage and divorce. Family sizes have reduced, around 80 per cent of Tunisians belong to the middle class and women now play an integral role in family, in wider social and economic contexts.

Exhibit 2.4
Main social indicators, 2000

Per capita income	TD2,720 (US$5,000 in terms of purchasing power parity)
Population (1999)*	9.442 million
Population growth*	1.12%
Life expectancy	72 years
Homeowners	78% of households
Electricity	94.6% of households
Drinkable water	75.2% of households
Schooling	99% of 6-year olds

Sources: Ministry of International Cooperation & Foreign Investment; *ONFP.

Legislation in education, health, social security, women's rights, children's rights and poverty alleviation have endorsed these changes, which are particularly unusual compared with the lack of such a complete range of policies in neighbouring North African countries.

The extent to which official policies and programmes have precipitated these changes or whether they are a response to organic cultural changes rooted in Tunisian society is a matter for some debate. However, the texture and dynamics of Tunisian society clearly reflect robust and far-sighted official actions, a central strand of which has been policies and programmes to moderate population growth. Exhibit 2.4 shows the main social indicators in 2000.

Population management

Tunisia has put the brakes on population growth. In the 1960s, in line with the late president Habib Bourguiba's modernist social concepts, contraceptives went on unrestricted sale, a health delivery system with particular emphasis on preventive services was introduced and the first National Family Planning Programme (NFPP) was introduced.

In 1973 the Office National de la Famille et de la Population (ONFP – National Board for Family and Population) was established. In the 1970s and 1980s the family planning programme was intensified, a basic healthcare policy introduced and the role of education in health and family planning heightened.

For the past decade, health and family planning policies and programmes have become part of a more holistic approach to social and economic development, with population policies integrated with strategies for environmental as well as regional, national and international development. According to the ONFP's director, Professor Nabiha Gueddana:

> It was essential to break the cycle between poverty and the birth rate – this went right back to the independence aim to make population growth a front-rank economic question … The key issue is quality of life. Tunisia is poorer in terms of resources than [neighbouring] Algeria, but Tunisia's GDP per head is now better than Algeria's, which reverses the past situation – and this is down to the effects of our social policies. Further, women's life is better, and that is good for society as a whole.

Apart from transforming the Tunisian family's traditional structure, moderate population growth has indeed contributed to the country's economic performance. According to ONFP's calculations, the Tunisian population would be more than 50 per cent larger than it was in 2000 with 15 million inhabitants if population growth had remained at the 1966 rate. Demographic control has, according to ONFP, spared the country from providing 650,000 jobs and about 770,000 places in education and has reduced the burden of spending on health and social security.

Active promotion of family planning has resulted in population growth slowing from 3 per cent in 1966 to 1.12 per cent in 1999. The average number of children per woman has decreased from 7.2 in 1966 to 2.2 in 1999.

ONFP continues to provide a framework within which health and education services are targeted at all regions and demographic groups. Demographic indicators reflect the effectiveness of sustained programmes implemented by the ONFP.

Falling birth rate

In 1999 Tunisia's population reached 9,442,000 (see Exhibit 2.5) having increased over the previous five years at an average of 131,400 inhabitants per year, despite continuous decreases in birth and mortality rates. Average population growth is expected to decrease still further to around 1 per cent a year.

Annual birth numbers began to fall in the late 1980s and the early 1990s (see Exhibit 2.6) to reach 160,000 births in 1999 against 200,000 births in 1994, despite an increase in the number of married women of reproductive age from 1.2 million in 1994 to nearly 1.3 million in 1999. According to the ONFP's Gueddana, this raises new questions of ageing:

> You could say that demographically, Tunisia is going through its golden age. The majority of the population is of working age, and after four decades of effort, is well educated. The demographics tell us that now is the time for the country to do something.

Exhibit 2.5
Population growth, 1956–99

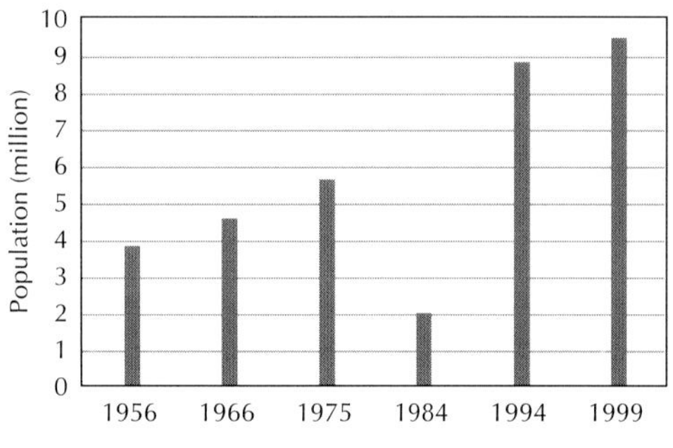

Source: ONFP.

Exhibit 2.6
Birth rate per 1,000 inhabitants

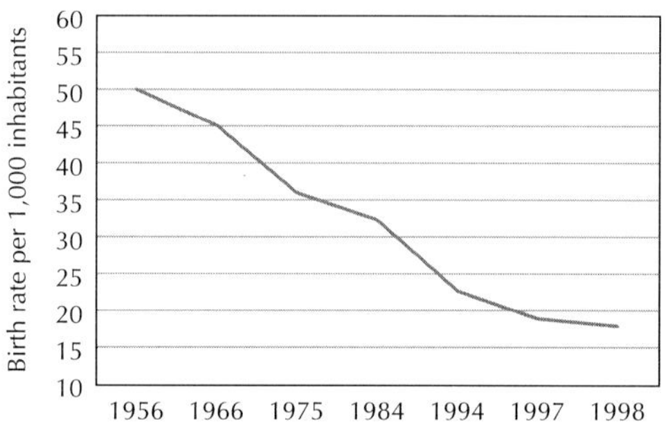

Source: ONFP.

A degree of reappraisal may now be necessary, Gueddana says:

> We need to get to a harmonious situation, where the age balance does not go too much in the other direction and that there is not too great a greying of the population, as has happened in Europe.

Exhibit 2.7
Trend of infant mortality, 1956–98

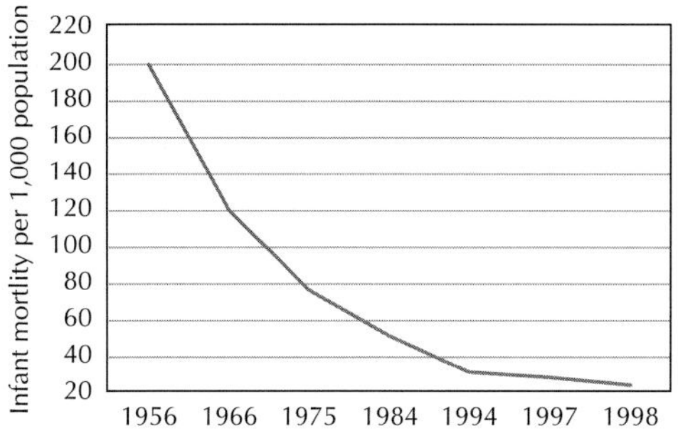

Source: ONFP.

Falling birth rates have been a more recent phenomenon in less developed areas of southern and west-central Tunisia. The birth rate fell by more that 25 per cent in the four years to 1998 in the administrative regions of Kairouan, Kasserine and Sidi Bouzid.

Infant mortality has also reduced significantly since the 1960s (see Exhibit 2.7), helped by a 'total health' policy in which qualified midwives and localised health centres play an important role.

Exhibit 2.8
Key population forecasts to 2030

Population growth	1995	2000	2005	2010	2015	2020	2025	2030
Total population (millions)	8.95	9.69	10.41	11.12	11.83	12.51	1.31	1.37
Age-group 0–14 years (%)	34.8	31 .3	28.3	26.5	25.1	24.2	23.1	22.1
Age-group 15–59 years (%)	56.9	60.1	63.1	64.7	65.1	64.6	63.8	62.9
Age-group 60 years and older (%)	8.3	8.6	8.6	8.8	9.7	11.2	13	15
Total fertility rate	2.87	2.53	2.27	2.10	2.10	2.10	2.10	2.10
Infant mortality	*1995*	*2000*	*2005*	*2010*	*2015*	*2020*	*2025*	*2030*
Male (per thousand)	33.8	26.2	20.3	16.1	13.2	11 .2	9.9	9.0
Female (per thousand)	27.2	20.9	16.2	12.7	10.4	8.8	7.7	7.0
Total (per thousand)	30.5	23.5	18.2	14.4	11.8	10.0	8.8	8.0
Life expectancy at birth	*1995*	*2000*	*2005*	*2010*	*2015*	*2020*	*2025*	*2030*
Male	69.5	70.5	71.4	72.0	72.6	73.0	73.4	73.7
Female	73.3	74.7	75.8	76.8	77.6	78.4	79.0	79.5
Total	71 .4	72.6	73.6	74.4	75.1	75.7	76.2	76.6

	1995–2000	*2000–05*	*2005–10*	*2010–15*	*2015–20*	*2020–25*	*2025–30*
Annual birth rate (per thousand)	21.7	20.0	18.7	17.9	17.0	15.9	15
Annual death rate (per thousand)	5.8	5.5	5.5	5.6	5.8	6	6.4
Annual growth rate (%)	1.6	1.5	1.3	1.2	1.1	1	0.9

Source: Institut National de la Statistique.

One net result of lower birth rates on Tunisia's demography has been a significant and continuous decline in the number of children under five years old. In 1966, children aged 0–4 years represented 18.6 per cent of the population but by 1999, this group accounted for just 9 per cent of inhabitants.

From an economic perspective, it is most significant that the active 15–59 year old population category has continuously increased, reaching 60.1 per cent in 1999 from 56.9 per cent in 1994 and just 48 per cent in 1966. Nevertheless, the Tunisian population remains young with an average age of 28.2 years in 1999.

The dominant active category is now well able to support Tunisia's younger (0–14 years) and older (over 60 years) populations at the moment. A new set of challenges will come as life expectancy lengthens and the proportion of older people relative to active inhabitants grows.

Life expectancy, particularly of women, has lengthened markedly (see Exhibit 2.8). In 1996 women could expect to live an average 15 years after the birth of their last child; by 1994 this period had lengthened to 35 years.

Information, education and communication services

For more than a decade considerable emphasis has been placed on the importance of information, health education and communications strategies to modify people's approach and behaviour in respect of reproduction. Consequently a generation of Tunisians has been exposed to family planning issues through ONFP's communications campaigns that have used television, radio, newspapers and magazines as well as posters and flyers.

Results from a four-year family planning and reproductive health programme that specifically targeted poorer areas in west-central and southern Tunisia highlights the effectiveness of ONFP's work. Various indicators of antenatal and postnatal health and of contraceptive use suggest that the agency's interventions can raise standards of women's health in poorer areas to levels similar to those in more developed areas. By the time the programme finished in 1999 the average use of contraceptives in the area had more than doubled (see Exhibit 2.9).

Exhibit 2.9

Population control and health data (% of population)

	1996	*1997*	*1999*
Contraceptive use average	50.1	54	64.2
Pregnancy control	69.1	77.6	89.3
Hospital delivery	59.8	76.2	95.3
Post-natal visits	68.5	62	85.6

Source: ONFP.

A leading role in population management

Tunisia is recognised as being at the forefront of interventions in population management in developing states. During a March 1999 visit to Tunisia, the then US first lady, Hillary Clinton described Tunisia as a model state and welcomed the republic's efforts to train people working in similar fields in 14 countries within the South-South partnership framework. Tunisia is honourary chairman of the body that aims to exchange expertise in population and development.

Information and education provided on a one-to-one basis in health centres, at voluntary associations and during home visits by reproductive health visitors has been fundamental to ONFP's strategy for creating awareness about family planning issues. Group health education sessions for men, women and young people are organised. Mobile educational teams provide social and health awareness services to urban and rural groups. Recently ONFP has taken to hiring girls from targeted regions, training them to disseminate health education messages and point people towards local family planning services. Health educators working for various associations and NGOs are also supported by ONFP.

Teachers, nurses and dignitaries are frequently enlisted to use their moral authority to convey ONFP's message in person or via the media. Young people are specifically trained to disseminate information to their peers in schools and other institutions.

Basic and secondary schools, vocational training centres and literacy centres include activities to raise awareness about family planning and reproductive health issues in their curricula. Learning aids and resources developed within ONFP's extensive media production facilities support these activities.

Production studios with live broadcasting and recording facilities for television and radio at ONFP's Tunis headquarters are impressive. These Japanese-funded facilities are part of the agency's Centre for the Production of Audio-visual Aids and Posters, created in 1994 to produce video films, photographs, transparencies, radio and television programmes and advertisements as well as printed posters and flyers and multimedia aids. The centre is fully equipped to produce these media in-house.

Significant financial support for the centre has been provided by Japan International Cooperation Agency (JICA), which collaborates with ONFD in several other integrated activities. These include contributing to the creation of a multimedia library and an audio-visual data bank on reproductive health, family planning and population and publishing a regular ONFP news bulletin. JICA also supports ONFP's Centre for Training and Research on Reproductive Health and Population. Research conducted by the centre includes studies into the medical and the demographic, social and behavioural aspects of reproductive health. Recent medical research has included studies of sterility among married couples, hormone transplants and intra-uterine devices. Non-medical research has, for example, examined men's attitudes to reproductive health and conducted a national family survey.

Each year, as well as training around 900 Tunisian staff in aspects of family planning, reproductive health and women's health, the centre also provides similar services to over 1,000 international trainees, mainly from other Arab and African nations. As well as its information, education and communications services, ONFP also delivers medical services. In 1999, ONPF provided over 2 million medical interventions compared with 41,517 in 1966. Each intervention is geared to meet a woman's specific family planning, antenatal, postnatal, gynaecological or post-fertility need or towards reducing the health risks of women's cancers and sexually transmitted diseases.

Women and education

Perhaps the most remarkable social transformation over the last generation – and one that has been bolstered by healthier, smaller families – is the changing role of women in Tunisian society. Consecration of women's rights in all fields, including education, health, employment, access to finance and participation in government and the workplace has marked this change.

- There are now more than 5,000 Tunisian businesswomen, 85 per cent of whom work in the industrial sector.
- The percentage of female members of parliament has increased from 4.2 per cent in 1989 to 11.5 per cent in 2000.
- Women have been represented in government since the 1980s. The percentage of female municipal councillors increased from 13.6 per cent in 1990 to 20.6 per cent in 1999.
- The percentage of female judges reached 24 per cent in 1998 as opposed to 10.5 per cent in 1984.
- In 2000, women accounted for 37 per cent of public sector and 46 per cent of manufacturing sector manpower, 28 per cent of university teaching staff and 33 per cent of doctors.

One of the main reasons for this transformation is improved access to education so that the percentage of women at various educational levels is equal or higher than men's percentage (see Exhibit 2.10). About 64 per cent of women are educated today as opposed to only 18 per cent in 1966.

Women's employment is also considered one of the most influential curbs on population growth and the spread of intolerant attitudes – an important factor in a country which has, in the past, feared the potentials for a radical Islamist backlash against modernising policies. Statistics show an increase in the percentage of economically active women from 18.7 per cent in 1975 to 24.6 per cent in 1999, despite the fact that women are of childbearing age at the same time as they fall into the economically active age category.

Exhibit 2.10

Breakdown of students by sex and education, 1999–2000 (%)

Educational level	*Females*	*Males*
Basic education	47.4	52.6
Secondary education	51.12	48.88
Higher education	50.37	49.63

Source: Institut National de la Statistique.

Later marriages and a consequent increase in the rate of celibacy have also contributed to the slowdown of population growth. The average marriage age is 31 years for men and 26 years for women. Around one in three men between 30 and 34 remain celibate as opposed to 16.2 per cent in 1966. In 1966 all women in this age category were married but today 15 per cent remain single, having preferred to pursue education and careers.

Human resources

The 2000 Report on Competitiveness in Africa, prepared by the World Economic Forum and Harvard University ranked Tunisia number one in terms of the quality of human resources on the continent. High standards in the workforce compared with other African countries are largely attributed to widespread access to quality education and training.

Labour costs are generally lower than those in Europe, at around half the cost of labour in the United Kingdom, about 25 per cent lower than in Portugal and about 15 per cent lower than in Turkey and Hungary. Social security costs are nearly half those in Turkey and on a par with those in Poland and Portugal.

Nevertheless, compared with its European trading partners and competitors, Tunisia faces skills gaps, unemployment at 15.5 per cent in 2000 remains high and labour structures remain rigid in the civil service and some competitive sectors.

Generating employment is therefore a priority in Tunisia's 10th Economic and Social Development Plan (2002–06) as it was in previous plans. The challenge will be to

Exhibit 2.11
Employment market breakdown (%)

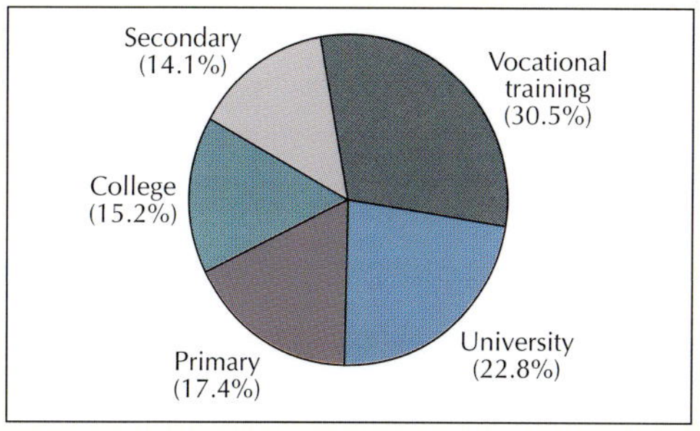

Source: Ministry of Economic Development.

Exhibit 2.12
Evolution of student numbers

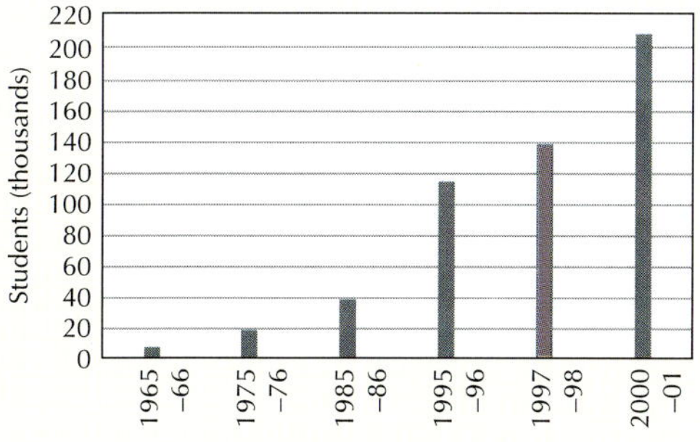

Source: Ministry of Higher Education.

Distribution of students in universities by major field, 1998–99

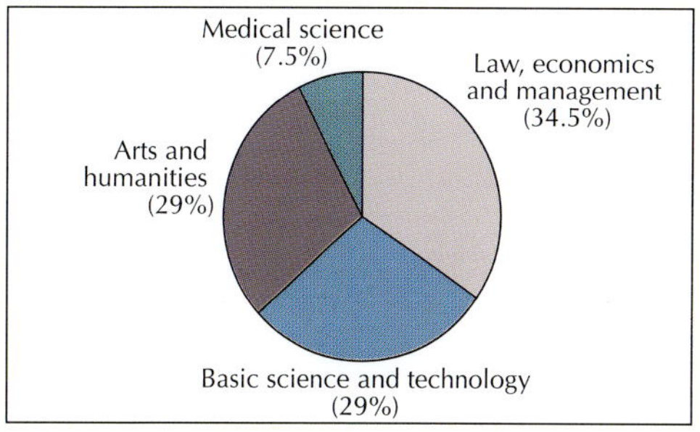

ensure that jobs are created at the same time as some apparently contradictory objectives, such as productivity gains and caps on public sector recruitment, are also achieved.

To ensure that future growth is accompanied by employment, the government has introduced several active labour market policies and training programmes to improve the match between the skills offered and demanded in the labour market. A more flexible workforce, able to respond to shifts in demand will also be needed.

Education

Today, one Tunisian out of four is being educated. This requires a budget of nearly 7 per cent of GDP but does mean that the workforce is, in a regional context, well educated. Around 53 per cent of job seekers have a university or professional qualification according to the Ministry of International Cooperation and Foreign Investment (see Exhibit 2.11).

University education

There has been a significant growth in the number of university students over recent years (see Exhibit 2.12). Around 175,000 students attend higher education establishments in Tunisia while around 15,000 students win places in foreign universities and colleges, particularly in the United States, Canada, France and Germany. Plans are also now under way to allow for the establishment of private universities.

Vocational training

Tunisia places considerable emphasis on vocational training, and plans to quadruple its enrolment capacity by 2003. The government may also meet up to 50 per cent of certain training costs incurred by companies and support continuous skills development programmes through a vocational training tax refund. Payments of up to 50 per cent of training costs may also be available for programmes of continual development in certain areas of technology.

Training is often developed and delivered in partnership with trade and professional bodies and those companies that require training services. Increasingly, trainees participate in courses that are based partly in the workplace and partly at a training centre.

In addition to several private vocational centres mainly operating in service-related activities, the Ministry of Vocational Training and Employment now has about 90 public centres across the country providing training in 164 subjects (see Exhibit 2.13).

Improving technological competencies required in the workplace is a priority. Tunisia aims to do this by establishing research and technical centres focused on several areas of business and bringing universities and companies closer together. These will focus on training quality and certification experts and on developing engineering and consulting skills.

Exhibit 2.13
Vocational training capacity

Field	*Sub-sector*	*Training capacity*
Buildings and related industries	Large projects	825
	Wood and Furnishing	1,282
	Air conditioning, & sanitary, cold industry	882
Textiles and clothing	Weaving	222
	Ready-made garments and hosiery	2 546
Leather and shoes	Shoes	560
	Fancy-leather	271
General mechanics and metal-building	Mechanical manufacturing	621
	Maintenance mechanics	352
	Welding	287
	Sheet-metal work and frame-work	624
	Plastic industry	170
	Drilling	105
	Agri-business	120
Electricity/electronics	Electro-mechanical industry	1,405
	Electronics	1,216
	Telecommunications	460
Services	Secretarial	400
	Management/accounting	640
Driving and maintenance	Vehicle driving	190
Agricultural and public works vehicles and machines	Driving working sites machines	14
	Vehicles and engines maintenance	1,319
	Engines maintenance	180
Tourism and hostelry	Entertainment	18
	Hostelry	282
Handicraft	Handicraft	60
Miscellaneous	Graphic arts	144
	Various services	285
	Paramedical services	568
Total		16,158

Source: Ministry of Vocational Training and Employment.

Infrastructure

Tunisia since independence has developed a modern infrastructure, reflected in everything from the capital's efficient and environmentally friendly Tunis Light Metro to plans for a number of new motorways. Details of many of these projects are covered in later chapters.

Transport

Road

Tunisia has 19,000 kilometres of roads, of which two-thirds or 12,200 kilometres are asphalted. There is, however, only one 140-kilometre motorway, which runs between Tunis and Msaken. Construction of a 60-kilometre highway linking Tunis to Bizerte is under way. There are plans for 850 kilometres of highway, including 450 kilometres that will be operational before 2010. The plans identify three routes:

- Tunis-M'Saken-Sfax-Gabès;
- Tunis-Medjez el Bab Bèz-Bousalem; and
- Enfidah-Kairouan-Gafsa.

Rail

Around 2,000 kilometres of railway lines transport 12 million tonnes of goods and 31.5 million passengers each year. This system is also in the process of being upgraded.

Shipping

There are eight commercial ports – Bizerte, La Goulette and Rades (both Tunis), Sousse, Sfax, Gabès, Zarzis and La Skhira – all equipped to handle roll-on roll-off ferries and container vessels. Annual traffic totals some 6,000 vessels and maritime goods traffic averages 23 million tonnes a year.

Scheduled shipping lines connect Tunis and Marseilles 10 times a week, Tunis and Genoa eight times a week, Tunis and Barcelona twice weekly and Tunis to Rotterdam, Bremen and Rouen two times a month.

Air

The country's air transport links are also in the process of being upgraded. There are 166 flights a week to Europe, served by 58 airlines representing 28 countries from seven international airports: Tunis, Monastir, Djerba, Tabarka, Tozeur, Sfax and Gafsa. Current airport capacity is 7.25 million passengers but will increase to 12.75 million with the expansion of Tunis, Monastir and Djerba airports.

Communications

Telecommunications in Tunisia are expanding rapidly, as discussed in later chapters. The

Tunisia has developed a modern infrastructure and is in the process of upgrading its transport links

national network is fully digitised and provides a broad range of products, including data transmittal, videotex, cellular telephone and internet services. Over 170 countries can be automatically direct dialled.

Telephone density will reach 14 lines per 100 inhabitants in 2001 and 20 lines per 100 inhabitants by 2004. This compares with 7.2 lines per 100 inhabitants in 1997. Investment in telecommunications is expected to reach TD1,335 million in the four years to 2001 compared with TD731 million in the four years to 1996.

3 *Economic management*

A prudent approach to building a new economy

Tunisia has, for some time, been one of the handful of Arab/African economies that enjoy investment grade ratings from international agencies. This fact reflects the country's success – rare in the region – at overcoming unpromising macroeconomic balances, which threatened a major debt crisis in the early 1980s. In the event, Tunisia did not join so many other developing countries on the rescheduling merry go-round, and has established an enviable repayments record. Instead, the administration set single-mindedly on a course of improving macroeconomic balances, while cautiously opening up the state-dominated economy to private enterprise and global markets. Since embarking on a process of structural adjustment in 1987 with the International Monetary Fund (IMF), policies introducing wide-ranging reforms have changed the roles of Tunisia's government, companies and consumers, and its relations with other countries in the macroeconomic balance. This process continues to this day.

Supply, demand and prices are increasingly determined by market forces instead of state interventions; the private sector frequently backed by foreign investment is now the major player in competitive sectors of the economy; and Tunisia has associated itself with the European Union to integrate itself in the global economy. Growth and export-oriented policies of economic liberalisation and diversification that have driven these dynamics over recent years continue today.

This long-term process of transition, and the struggle to overcome administrative blockages, is described by Economic Development Minister Abdellatif Saddem:

> The Tunisian state's traditional role was to authorise, and even to punish. This tendency towards authorisation became rigid and pervasive. It has taken a lot of time for the administration to learn the need for it to content itself to setting norms and controlling infractions. But now, we seem without doubt to have passed that line – although we still have to watch that bureaucracy does not become too over-weaning. After all, what you throw out of the door can still come back in through the window.

Saddem sees this freeing up of the business and social environment as a key role for the leadership and civil service:

> President Ben Ali listens to deepest Tunisia [la Tunisie profonde], and this was reflected in 2000 by the decision to eliminate a range of authorisations. There are now only about 40 per cent of these authorisations left in place, and these are mainly linked to strategic sectors such as health and security. Otherwise even the most deeply rooted old concessions have gone, such as the state's control over the automobiles market. Take the case of cars, now for imports the state merely issues specifications in a cahiers de charge, and then the business can be expedited quickly.

A role for market forces

Tunisia's strong economic performance, especially by regional standards, is rooted in prudent and balanced macroeconomic management that aims for continued fiscal consolidation and control over inflation, backed by a sound record of investment in social and physical infrastructure. According to Industry Minister Moncef Ben Abdallah:

> Our policy is based on defining the limits of government, with strong encouragement for the private sector to change the overall balance of an economy that was traditionally state-led ... There is now an open investment environment; trade is 90 per cent liberalised; and most prices are fixed by the market. Even where there are still some subsidies – on the most socially sensitive goods such as wheat, cous cous and edible oils – these prices are also slowly being raised to market levels. The role of the [state subsidies body] Caisse Générale de Compensation has gradually diminished, to a stage where it could just provide some essential seasonal support.

The tax system has undergone significant adjustments, notably through reforms to indirect taxes, such as the introduction of value-added tax (VAT). Implementation of effective tax measures has been, and will remain, an important counterweight to the decline in trade tariffs, duties and other taxes as a result of freer trading terms, particularly with Europe. Tunisia's association agreement with the European Union – discussed below – includes provision for the progressive withdrawal of customs duties on goods imported from Tunisia's dominant trading partner. This could have a significant potential impact for the state budget, as well as for local companies who must adapt quickly to function in a much more competitive environment.

Reforms to the banking system include the freeing of interest rates and the introduction of banking legislation that determines prudential standards and solvency ratios. Other reforms in the financial system include the privatisation of the stock exchange and the establishment of a Capital Market Council (CMF).

A new investment code provides a sound framework for domestic and foreign investors, while state-owned companies in several competitive sectors have or will be part of Tunisia's privatisation programme. Encouraged by more liberal exchange, trade and regulatory regimes, the private sector has expanded rapidly is the export and tourism sectors.

The investment trend is upward as shown in Exhibit 3.1.

Exhibit 3.1
Investment trend, 1996–2001

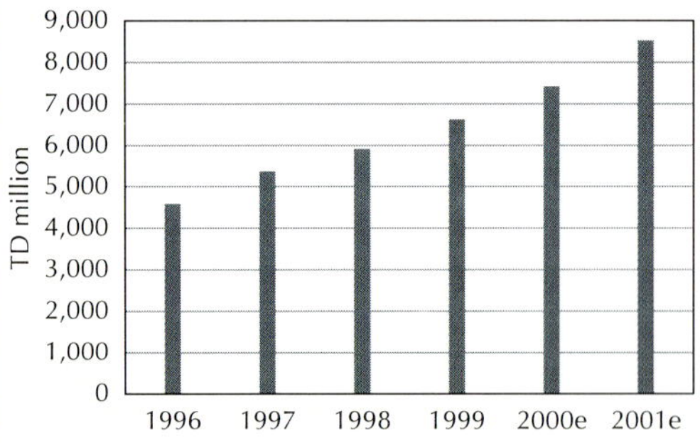

Source: Banque Centrale de Tunisie.

Upgrading the domestic economy

Several strands make up the country's policy for upgrading and improving quality and performance in the industrial sector, including a raft of educational and vocational training programmes. A member of the World Trade Organisation, Tunisia was also the first country on the Mediterranean's southern rim to conclude an association agreement with the European Union, the main component of which is the progressive establishment of a free-trade area. In this context, Tunisia has initiated a programme of multi-sectoral reforms aimed at laying the foundations for a solid, diversified and competitive economy capable of adapting to the new international environment.

These basic reforms aim to eliminate imbalances impeding deregulation and have a positive impact on prices, commerce, the tax system, the investment incentive system, the banking sector, the stock market and the capital market.

Ministry of Finance, Tunis

Exhibit 3.2

Incomes and savings, 1996–2001(E) (TD million)

	1996	*1997*	*1998*	*1999*	*2000 (E)*	*2001 (E)*
Gross national disposable income	18,862.5	20,734.1	22,553.9	24,851.1	26,976.2	29,483
Domestic savings	4,279.1	4,847.8	5,299.2	6,078	6,596.4	7,299.8
Population ('000s)	9,024.8	9,153.8	9,275.8	9,392.3	9,508.8	9,607.6
Per capita income	2,030	2,265	2,431	2,645	2,837	3,068

Source: Ministry of Economic Development.

Sustained growth and much improved living conditions for most Tunisians – despite the country's modest natural resources – have resulted in some observers citing Tunisia as a model of economic management for developing countries. As Exhibit 3.2 shows, domestic demand has been sustained by the rising real incomes of a burgeoning middle class. This growth is the result of coherent and prudent macroeconomic policies, pursued in a medium-term perspective. Combined with progressive social policies, this approach has produced remarkable growth rates, as well as some significant advances in social indicators.

Positive indicators

Several economic indicators highlight the efficacy of Tunisia's economic management over recent years (see Exhibit 3.3) while the sum of recent indicators point to the stabilisation of a sustainable macroeconomic framework:

- Sustained GDP growth at an average rate of 5.4 per cent at constant prices was achieved over the first four years of the 9th Plan, an indicative document setting out the government's goals for the economy's development in 1997–2001.
- Inflation was reduced to 2.7 per cent in 1999, the lowest level since 1972.
- Increases in investment at a sustained annual rate of 13.5 per cent have seen Tunisia's investment ratio raised from 23.2 per cent of GDP in 1996 to 25.2 per cent in 1999.
- The savings rate has risen from 23.7 per cent to 25.4 per cent in the four years to 1999.

A robust performance

Tunisia's economy proved its robustness in 2000. Despite severe drought conditions that resulted in poor agricultural output, and consequently higher food imports and prices, the authorities and the IMF remained confident that real GDP growth would still reach 5 per cent for the year. Excluding agriculture, GDP grew by an estimated 6 per cent in 2000, due to solid export performance and strong domestic demand.

Exhibit 3.3

Key domestic economic indicators, 1996–99 (TD million unless otherwise indicated)

	1996	1997	1998	1999	% change 1998/97	% change 1999/98
Gross domestic product (in 1990 constant prices)	14,009	14,771	15,475	16,441	4.8	6.2
GDP excluding agriculture and fishing	11,971	12,673	13,398	14,133	5.7	5.5
Value-added of agriculture and fishing	2,038	2,098	2,077	2,308	-1.0	11.1
GDP at current prices	19,066	20,898	22,600	24,777	8.1	9.6
GDP deflator (1990=100)	136.1	141.5	146.0	150.7	3.2	3.2
GNP per capita (TD)	2,001.4	2,174	2,330	2,531	7.1	8.6
GNP per capita (in US dollars)	2,039	1,958	2,036	2,114	4.0	3.8
Gross national available income (GNAI)	18,863	20,734	22,554	24,851	8.8	10.1
Overall domestic consumption	14,583	15,886	17,255	18,773	8.6	8.8
Public consumption	(2,965)	(3,295)	(3,541)	(3,853)	(7.5)	(8.8)
Private consumption	(11,618)	(12,591)	(13,714)	(14,920)	(8.9)	(8.8)
Average consumption/GNAI %[1]	77.3	76.6	76.5	75.7	-0.1	-0.8
Gross national savings	4,279	4,848	5,299	6,078	9.3	14.7
National savings rate (in % of GNP)[1]	23.7	24.4	24.5	25.6	0.1	1.1
Gross fixed capital formation	4,422	5,153	5,592	6,255	8.5	11.8
Public sector	(2,058.6)	(2,496.7)	(2,619)	(2,991)	(4.9)	(14.2)
Private sector	(2,363.7)	(2,656.7)	(2,972.7)	(3,264)	(11.9)	(9.8)
Investment rate (in % of GDP)[1]	23.2	24.7	24.7	25.2	0.0	0.5
Consumer price index (1990=100)	137.4	142.4	146.8	150.8	3.1	2.7
of which: foodstuffs	137.0	142.8	146.7	150.0	2.7	2.3
Jobs creation ('000 jobs)[2]	55.3	58.0	61.0	63.0	5.2	3.3

[1] Variations in percentage points.

[2] In non-agricultural activities.

Sources: Banque Centrale de Tunisie; Ministries of Economic Development and Finance and INS.

Exhibit 3.4

Fiscal balances, 1996–99

	1996	1997	1998	1999	Variations in % 1998/97	Variations in % 1999/98
Fiscal pressure as % of GDP	19.8	20.2	21.1	21.0	0.9	-0.1
Ordinary budget balance (TD mn)	442.7	337.7	605.2	706.0	79.2	16.7
Investment expenditures (TD mn)	1,555.1	1,647.1	1,881.6	2,100.5	-0.8	18.7
Budget deficit (excluding debt) as % of GDP	4.3	4.3	1.3	3.5	-3.0	2.2
Total state debt/GDP ratio (%)	55.6	62.3	58.8	60.6	-3.5	1.8

Sources: Banque Centrale de Tunisie; Ministries of Economic Development and Finance and INS.

Exhibit 3.5

Key external economic indicators, 1996–99 (TD million unless otherwise indicated)

	1996	*1997*	*1998*	*1999*	*Variations in %* *1998/97*	*1999/98*
Export cover % (exports fob/imports cif)	71.6	69.9	68.7	69.2	-1.2	0.5
Trade deficit	2,127	2,646	2,971	3,094	12.3	4.5
Tourist earnings	1,413	1,565	1,713	1,950	9.4	14.1
Remittances	798	846	902	1,020	6.6	13.1
Current deficit	499.6	680.4	774	535.8	13.7	-30.8
Current deficit as % of GDP	2.6	3.3	3.4	2.2	0.1	-1.2
Net capital inflows	841.1	947.8	467.5	1,269.2	-50.7	241.6
Balance of payments	+386	+372	-213	+818	-586	1,031
Debt service ratio (%)	17.6	16.4	16.5	15.7	-0.1	-0.8
External debt as % of GNAI	51.0	52.2	48.1	51.5	-4.1	3.4

Sources: Banque Centrale de Tunisie;. Ministries of Economic Development and Finance, INS and IMF.

Macroeconomic policies employed during 2000 should also enable Tunisia to counter the negative effects of high world oil prices, including public spending on petroleum price supports. These costs should be offset by significant increases in tax revenue and in some non-tax revenues. The budget deficit in 2000 was projected at around 3.5 per cent of GDP (excluding privatisation proceeds and grants), similar to its 1999 level (see Exhibit 3.4). Monetary policy was also largely on target, in so far as credit and monetary aggregates have grown roughly in line with GDP.

The external current account deficit (3.2 per cent of GDP in 2000) widened relative to 1999, again due mainly to sharp increases in the volume of imports and the rise in oil prices (the energy balance is slightly negative in volume terms).

Sound economic management has resulted in Tunisia's constantly improving international credit rating, enabling it to borrow on the international markets in 2000 at a much lower margin (130 basis points on a 10-year yen issue) than in 1999 (280 basis points on a 10-year euro issue).

Access to international financial markets has allowed Tunisia to build up a level of reserves equivalent to three months of imports and 90 per cent of short-term financial liabilities.

Key external indicators are shown in Exhibit 3.5.

A growing role for services

Agricultural output was expected to rebound in 2001 and the government sees GDP growing by 6.2 per cent in 2001 (see Exhibit 3.6). It forecast that the agriculture sector would expand by 6.5 per cent in 2001 with a strong increase in cereals output to 1.8 million tonnes in 2001, up from 1.09 million in 2000. It projected that the services sector would grow 8 per cent from

Exhibit 3.6

Medium-term growth scenario

	2000	*2001*	*2002*	*2003*	*2004*	*2005*	*2006*
Real GDP growth (%)	5.0	6.2	6.1	6.3	6.5	6.6	6.7
Agriculture[1] (%)	-1.0	6.5	4.5	4.5	4.5	4.5	4.5
Non-agriculture (%)	6.0	6.2	6.4	6.6	6.8	6.9	7.0
Unemployment rate (%)	15.5	15.1	14.6	13.9	13.1	12.2	11.2
Inflation (%)	3.0	2.9	2.7	2.7	2.2	2.2	2.1
Real export growth[2] (%)	5.9	6.5	5.8	6.4	6.0	6.6	6.5
Gross national savings (% of GDP)	24.5	25.0	25.4	26.1	26.7	27.4	28.0
Central government (% of GDP)	4.9	4.7	4.8	5.1	5.5	5.8	6.1
Rest of the economy (% of GDP)	19.7	20.3	20.6	20.9	21.2	21.5	21.9
Gross investment (% of GDP)	27.7	27.9	28.4	28.8	29.6	30.1	30.7
Central government (% of GDP)	4.4	4.6	4.5	4.5	4.5	4.5	4.5
Rest of the economy (% of GDP)	23.3	23.4	23.9	24.3	25.1	25.6	26.2
Savings-investment gap (% of GDP)	-3.2	-3.0	-3.0	-2.8	-2.8	-2.7	-2.6
Central government (% of GDP)	0.4	0.1	0.3	0.6	1.0	1.3	1.6
Rest of the economy (% of GDP)	-3.6	-3.1	-3.3	-3.4	-3.8	-4.1	-4.3
Memorandum items:							
Balance of the consolidated central government (% of GDP)[3]	-2.9	-2.5	-2.3	-2.0	-1.7	-1.3	-1.0
Consolidated central government (% of GDP)[2]	-1.7	1.0	0.8	-0.6	-0.9	-0.6	-0.4
Gross fixed capital formation (% of GDP)	26.2	26.3	26.8	27.2	28.0	28.6	29.2

[1] Based on average growth of agricultural output from 2002 onwards.

[2] Goods and non-factor services.

[3] Includes the social security system and grants; excludes privatisation proceeds.

Notes

* If the social security surplus is factored in, the consolidated deficit comes to 2.9 per cent of GDP in 2000, compared with 2.6 per cent in 1999, when the social security surplus was exceptionally large.
* During the period 2001–06, the scenario assumes a cumulative growth in exports of goods (excluding petroleum) of 50 per cent, compared with a growth of export markets of 44 per cent.
* Even with the projected increase in the rate of private saving, a reduction in the fiscal deficit to 1 per cent of GDP by 2006 would be necessary to maintain the current account deficit below 3 per cent of GDP.

Source: IMF Preliminary conclusions of the 2000 Article IV mission, 29 October 2000.

an estimated 7 per cent in 2000, contributing 2.9 per cent in GDP growth in 2001. These indicators say much for the performance of the Tunisian economy – old mainstays such as agriculture remain of major importance, but newer sectors such as services are quickly playing a more important role in the economy. The new economy, including a range of services and technology-based industries, has yet to grow to the same extent as in Europe and North

America, but its development has been much more marked in Tunisia than in most comparable emerging markets.

Investment also continues to climb, as shown in Exhibit 3.3, while the government sees the private sector increasing its share in planned investment to 55 per cent in 2001 from 52.6 per cent in 2000. The inflation rate is forecast at around 3.0 for 2001, roughly the same rate in 2000 (see Exhibit 3.6). Inflation had fallen to 2.7 per cent in 1999 and although the underlying rate remained stable in 2000, higher food and petroleum prices pushed the overall rate upwards.

Rising up on the shore of Lac Nord is the new Berges du Lac mixed development

Medium-term outlook

Tunisia's macroeconomic policy is predicated on the inseparability of economic and social development, but in the medium-term and in Tunisia's 10th Plan (2002–06), added emphasis on employment is required. Social gains cited by the authorities as a result of policies so far include improvements in Tunisians' incomes and purchasing power. Less than 6 per cent of Tunisians were classed as impoverished in 1999 when substandard housing accounted for only 1.2 per cent of total stock. In the same year 63,000 jobs were created.

However, the progressive increase in real GDP growth to 6.7 per cent by 2006 envisaged in medium-term forecasts prepared by the IMF would necessarily result from anticipated productivity gains and investments in human capital. The average growth rate in employment would be close to 3.5 per cent a year and the fixed investment rate would rise from the current level of 26 per cent of GDP to 29 per cent of GDP by 2006. Assuming an average annual increase of 80,000 people into the labour force, this scenario forecasts a drop in unemployment from 15.5 per cent in 2000 to 11 per cent by 2006.

The macroeconomic framework presented in Exhibit 3.7 aims to stimulate higher growth, improvements in real wages and living standards and gradually reduce the rate of unemployment.

Achieving these objectives will call for higher growth in the volume of exports, averaging around 6.25 per cent in 2001-06. This will require exporters to become even more competitive to gain and retain positions in European and world markets. If Tunisia does this it would indicate the country had realised its ambition to create a market economy that fully integrates with global economies.

Productivity gains must be made

Whether this ambition is reached, however, is dependent on productivity gains. The IMF prescribes three further preconditions for gains:

- Financial structures need to be strengthened and the credit culture improved, so as to mobilise private savings more effectively and allocate capital to the most productive uses.
- The pace of economic liberalisation and private sector involvement in the economy needs to accelerate in order to generate the investment necessary to manage productivity gains.
- Labour market reforms are needed to ensure that growth is rich in employment.

Industry Minister Ben Abdallah believes the transition to a more open economy has already allowed Tunisian industry to compete more effectively in global markets:

> Local industry has been doing well since the European accord was signed in 1996 – and this was reflected in figures for 2000, when production rose by around 10 per cent, exports were 14 per cent-plus higher. Investment is also growing, helped by a more dynamic industrial base and the *mise à niveau* programme. These figures should be even better in 2002–06, according to our studies for the tenth plan.

For macroeconomic policy, the challenge is to maintain internal and external equilibrium while adapting to the structural changes in the economy.

Public finances

Recent state budgets have been marked by several factors, including the sustained effort to secure income to offset custom tariffs being phased out under the Association Agreement with the European Union and sporadic shortfalls in income from privatisation. Renewed focusing of public expenditure on investment, particularly for economic and social sectoral infrastructure has also determined the management of public finances.

The government plans to increase spending for 2001 by TD310 million, or 2.9 per cent, from TD10.51 billion in projected expenditure for 2000. Total public debt repayments are projected at TD3.94 billion in 2001, 2.7 per cent lower than planned debt payments for 2000.

The bulk of state spending is on operating expenditure, capital goods acquisition and the granting of loans (see Exhibit 3.7). Operating expenditure includes the costs of pay and salaries, which is generally accepted to be too high. In 1999, the public sector wage bill accounted for about two-thirds of operating expenditure, equivalent to 10.8 per cent of GDP.

In 1999 expenditure grew faster than it did in the previous year and income dropped, mainly due to the lack of privatisation deals. This meant the budget deficit exclusive of debt retirement reached TD875 million or 3.5 per cent of GDP, compared with 1.3 per cent of GDP in 1998 and 4.2 per cent in 1997. The 1999 deficit was covered by TD525 million in net domestic resources and TD350 million in net external resources (see Exhibit 3.8).

A deficit of 2.7 per cent is estimated for 2000, a year in which the proceeds of privatisation proceeds increased fivefold over receipts from the sale of state assets in 1999. In 2001, the government aims for a budget deficit of TD700 million (2.4 per cent of the GDP), with the budget projected at TD10.82 billion, 2.9 per cent up from 2000.

If Tunisia is to achieve the anticipated medium-term deficit reduction the administration will need to tackle some existing burdens on the budget. As well as trimming the public sector wage bill, savings are also possible on foodstuff subsidies, which account for 0.7 per cent of GDP.

A broader tax base is also required to offset the lower revenues resulting from reduced trade tariffs. The 2001 budget sets Tunisia on this course. Taxes estimated at TD6.105 billion account for 56.4 per cent of the government's projected receipts in 2001 compared with TD5.624 billion in estimated tax revenues for 2000. The government said the increased tax revenues for 2001 will be generated mostly by improved tax collection, not tax increases.

Tax revenues have been rising, although growth has been progressively slower as customs duties are phased out (see Exhibit 3.9). The increase of the VAT rate from 17 to 18 per cent accounted for the steep rise in VAT receipts in 1998.

2001 budget

The 2001 budget also cut the deficit to TD700 million, or 2.4 per cent of GDP. This compares with TD750 million (2.7 per cent of GDP) in 2000 and TD910 million (3.6 per cent), according to government data. The

Exhibit 3.7

State budget expenditure, 1997–99

	1997	*1998*	*1999*
Operating capital goods and loans granting expenditure	5,278	5,580	6,202
Operating expenditure	3,634	3,899	4,102
Capital goods and loan granting	1,647	1,681	2,100
Debt service	2,850.4	3,078	3,154.5
Principal	2,061.7	2,308	2,315.6
Interest	788.7	770	838.9
Total	8,125.4	8,658	9,356.5

Source: Banque Centrale de Tunisie.

Exhibit 3.8

Financing the deficit, 1997–99

	1997	*1998*	*1999*
Net domestic financing	344	278	525
Internal borrowing resources	1,874	1,806	1,656
Debt redemption	-1,638	-1,693	-1,566
Financing from Treasury resources	108	165	435
Net foreign financing	543	10	350
External borrowing resources	1,167	625	1,095
Debt redemption	-624	-615	-745
Total	887	288	875

Source: Banque Centrale de Tunisie.

Exhibit 3.9

Tax revenues, 1997–99

	1997	*1998*	*1999*
Ordinary fiscal revenues	4,036	4,553	4,923
Direct taxes	1,110	1,286	1,384
Income taxes	681.2	777	893
of which: payroll taxes	482.1	548	644
Corporate tax	429	514	491
Levies and indirect taxes	2,926	3,267	3,539
Custom taxes and duties	704	714	687
VAT	1,170	1,437	1,625
Consumption taxes	722	775	858
Other levies and indirect taxes	330	341	369
Treasury funds tax revenue	192	210	284
Total	4,228	4,763	5,207

Source: Banque Centrale de Tunisie.

government plans to increase spending for 2001 by TD310 million, or 2.9 per cent, from TD10.51 billion in projected expenditure for 2000.

Taxes, estimated at TD6.105 billion, account for 56.4 per cent of projected receipts in 2001 compared with TD5.624 billion in estimated tax revenues for 2000. The government said the increased tax revenues for 2001 will be generated mostly by improved tax collection, not tax increases.

Non-tax earnings in some areas have reduced significantly. Oil revenues have fallen due to reduced output from Tunisia's declining oil fields, although appreciation of the dollar and stronger oil prices in 2000 softened the effect of lower production. Earnings from some state-owned industrial and commercial operations have fallen in recent years. Other non-fiscal revenues include royalties from Algerian gas transported across Tunisian territory, loan interest collection, payments from social security funds, loan principal collection and grants.

For 2001, Tunisia is budgeting TD985 million more revenues from privatisation receipts, foreign donations and estimated profits from state-owned firms. The balance of TD3.730 billion would be borrowed domestically and derived from external debt.

Prospects for external borrowing

Since its first intervention on the international capital market in 1994, Tunisia has accessed around TD3 billion, thereby contributing to the improvement of its debt structure. Borrowing from international markets is forecast at TD2.90 billion, according to the 2001 budget text. Tunisia has considerable credibility in international markets, and has borrowed from several sources (see Exhibit 3.10). The government projected a cut in borrowing from local and foreign markets to 59.3 per cent of the GDP in 2001 compared with an estimated 59.6 per cent in 2000.

Exhibit 3.10
External financing sources, 1998 and 1999

	1998	*1999*
Bilateral	278	284
France	84	109
United States	55	0
Japan	36	117
Other	103	58
Multilateral	347	527
World Bank	126	201
African Development Bank	80	180
European Investment Bank	91	87
Arab Fund for Economic & Social Development	32	42
Other	18	17
International capital market	0	284
Total	625	1,095

Source: Banque Centrale de Tunisie.

Benchmark financing and external debt management

An ability to meet international obligations has helped improve international perceptions of Tunisian risk. When it was revealed in September 2000 that it would issue an innovative global Samurai bond, Banque Centrale de Tunisie (BCT – the central bank) former governor Mohamed Beji Hamda

Exhibit 3.11
Total external debt, 1996–2000

	1996	*1997*	*1998*	*1999*	*2000*
Total external debt (TD millions?)	9,620.0	10,820.0	10,857	12,795	13,825
Rate of indebtedness as % of GDP	50.5	51.8	48.0	51.5	51.3
Debt service (TD millions)	1,599.1	1,689.3	1,791.2	1,856.6	2,400.0
Debt service / current receipts (%)	17.6	16.4	16.5	15.7	18.1
Debt service ratio[1] (%)	19.9	18.4	18.6	17.8	20.5

[1] Repayments as % of goods and services exports.

Source: Banque Centrale de Tunisie.

(governor until January 2001) noted that Tunisia had reimbursed in February and March about TD500 million of Japanese loans earlier in the year.

The bond deal is one of the first global Samurai bond deals to accommodate both Japanese and non-Japanese investors, which also suggests that Tunisia's financial community is learning some sophisticated operations. Moody's Investors Service assigned Baa3 ratings to the ¥35 billion global Samurai bond, due in 2010, and the Y15 billion global bond, due in 2030. The ratings correspond to the Baa3 foreign currency country ceiling previously assigned by Moody's Investors Service to Tunisia. The outlook for the ratings is positive. The bond is rated BBB by Standard & Poor's (S&P).

Tunisia is able to set new benchmarks, despite still retaining a sizeable external debt. This debt is generally sustainable, although the country has been under pressure from the high volume of drawings and the appreciation of currencies in which debt is handled against the Tunisian dinar. Although external debt has risen, the rate of indebtedness as a percentage of GDP has been gradually reducing over recent years (see Exhibit 3.11).

The governor's view

Following more than a decade at the helm of Banque Centrale de Tunisie, Mohammad Béji Hamda (governor until January 2001) told the authors of this book that debt and other external balances are now well under control – a marked change from the situation in the late-1980s, when Tunisia was already embarked on reform but only aspired to the sort of external indicators it can report today:

> Today, the question of debt management is not solely focused on managing difficult indicators. Rather while we still need to raise debt, the determining element in this is the need to finance imports for growth – new debt must be reserved for revenue-generating projects and reflect the need to assure foreign currency resources which create jobs.

Total external debt is now equivalent to around 40 per cent of GDP and the debt service ratio has fallen to around 16 per cent in 2000 – although it will rise to around 18 per cent in 2001 as some major repayments fall due. According to Béji Hamda, this relatively sound position is due to a long process of debt management:

> We have followed the global experience, starting with big bilateral borrowing, then a focus on multilateral lending and then, from the mid-1990s, private and other forms of financing as Tunisia's economy improved and we became ineligible for soft lending. As this happened, we evolved a strategy to become established in the markets – it was necessary to go in stages, and we focused on Japan, because at that stage Japan's was the most liquid market.

A stream of samurai bonds have followed, with BCT focusing on the Tokyo market to raise funds – but not exclusively. When the opportunities have been right – for example, to enter the Euro syndications or Yankee bond markets – Tunisia has taken them.

> Japan gave the easiest access, and between 1995 and 1997 we undertook six Samurai operations raising around TD1 billion; this helped establish Tunisia with foreign investors – we became better known. In July 1997 we were able to raise a 30-year Yankee on excellent terms, and more was to follow, but then the Asian financial crisis intervened. We could have borrowed subsequently but, with an established Samurai benchmark of 15 years at 130 basis points (bp) we didn't want to put our benchmarks in jeopardy. Consequently, we didn't come back until mid-2000, when we raised the global Samurai.

Further borrowing is envisaged in 2001, with Tunisia looking to set new benchmarks with repayments set below 200 basis points. Obtaining the optimum market conditions is essential for these operations to go ahead. Plans for a private placement, which had been expected to come to market in late 2000, were pulled due to market turbulence, Béji Hamda said.

After years when the debt burden was exacerbated by a lack of active debt management techniques, BCT has developed an active management programme, using a range of hedges. With yen borrowing so important, BCT has become experienced in hedging this debt into US dollars. BCT's dealing room now has 15 fully trained staff, and systems to keep control of market fluctuations which might impact on the debt stock.

Debt repayments

Debt service payments absorb around 20 per cent of goods and services exports. Public and publicly-guaranteed debt accounts for about 80 per cent of total debt, and consists mostly of medium- and long-term maturity debts. Short-term debt is mostly contracted by the private sector. The remaining debt consists of short-term liabilities in the banking system but around half of these liabilities are foreign currency or dinar convertible deposits of non-residents in the banking sector. In the opinion of BCT, this does not make Tunisia's external position vulnerable. BCT and the Finance Ministry work closely to collate data.

Inflation control and maintenance of foreign reserves

Control over inflation has exceeded expectations outlined in Tunisia's 9th Plan (1997–2001). The plan projected annual inflation of 3.7 per cent for 1997–2001. In the first three years of the plan inflation averaged 3.2 per cent but it dropped to 2.7 per cent in 1999, the lowest level since 1992. For a country with such ambitions to enter the European economic area, such indicators are very encouraging – they would place Tunisia comfortably within the so-called Maastricht criteria.

Notwithstanding pressure from high oil and foodstuff prices during 2000, the inflation rate was contained at around 3 per cent. Excluding foodstuffs, the rate of inflation was reduced over the first seven months of the year to 1.8 per cent compared with 3.3 per cent in the same period of the previous year. High production in agriculture and fishing had led to low inflation in 1999.

A key driver of policies to control inflation is the authorities' aim to keep rates in line with countries with which Tunisia trades or competes. The 1999 inflation rate was close to those recorded in several European countries including Greece and Spain but remained higher than inflation rates recorded in Tunisia's three main trading partners, France, Italy and Germany as well as Morocco.

Control over inflation has been improved through the pursuit of rigorous monetary policies, enhanced competition, intensified economic controls, improved productivity, targeted campaigns to encourage traders to keep prices at moderate levels and more efficient and better supervised distribution channels, particularly through better organised wholesale markets. Keeping prices low has also involved rationalising consumption, especially hire purchases, through the setting up of specialised structures dealing in loans.

Gradually reducing import prices for most products in the two years to 1999 had a positive effect on production inputs. This factor, along with improved productivity, has also contributed to keeping prices down and improved competitiveness. Lower prices have in turn helped strengthen economic fundamentals by improving purchasing power and increasing competition, both of which help develop exports and strengthen Tunisia's case for attracting foreign investment and mobilising foreign capital.

As well as the external forces of higher oil and food prices in 2000, longer-term factors that have loosened the authorities' control over inflation include insufficient competitiveness in some economic activities, price adjustments on items such as cereals, and growing consumption.

Meanwhile Tunisia has generally built foreign currency reserves over recent years, but there have been some significant variations. Net assets in foreign currency reserves amounted to TD2.75 billion at end-December 1999, corresponding to 98 days of imports compared with TD2.03 billion, corresponding to 77 days of imports at end-December 1998 (see Exhibit 3.12).

However, reserves in July 2000 amounted to just TD1.74 billion compared with TD2.02 billion for the same month in 1999, corresponding to 57 and 74 days of imports respectively. In August 2000, reserves recovered and amounted to TD2.60 billion, slightly up from TD2.51 billion in August 1999, corresponding to imports of 83 and 92 days respectively. These fluctuations are due to a number of factors, including Tunisia's schedule of debt repayments.

Exhibit 3.12
Trend of reserves, 1994–99

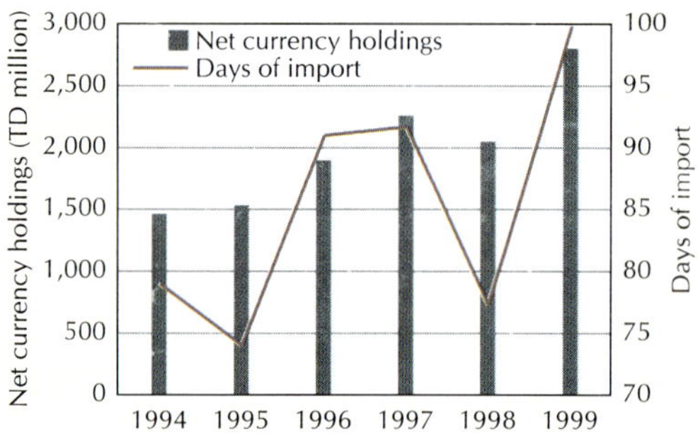

Source: Banque Centrale de Tunisie.

Currency management and exchange controls

Flexible exchange rate management remains a key element of macroeconomic policy.
The dinar exchange rate is determined freely on the foreign exchange market. The market is created between deposit banks in Tunis, including offshore banks operating on behalf of their resident customers. BCT intervenes on this market and publishes the interbank exchange rate of currencies and banknotes at the latest the following day.

Importers and exporters may cover themselves against exchange risk on the forward interbank market. Forward rates are freely negotiated between operators and the counterpart bank.

The Tunisian dinar has been convertible for current transactions since 1992 and, as a result, the transfer of capital and profits are free. This includes remuneration of profit-making shares, dividends, directors' fees and interest on loans. Transfers related to commercial transactions and associated operations are free, as are production-related transfers.

Tunisian exporters have facilities to pay their suppliers directly in currency and may keep foreign currency accounts for this purpose. Since 1993, transfers relating to these payments to suppliers are free and are not subject to prior authorisation from BCT.

For current foreign trade operations domiciled with an approved intermediary there is no exchange control.

- For capital operations there are some restrictions, although several bilateral agreements provide freedom of transfer of dividends or of the capital element in a partially or fully liquidated investment.
- Partly or fully export-oriented resident corporates may invest abroad to support their exporting efforts.
- Banks and corporates may borrow in foreign currencies for activities within the limits of TD10 and TD3 million per year respectively.
- Foreign investors may take portfolio positions of at least 50 per cent in listed or unlisted Tunisian corporates.

Euro turbulence

The authorities have adapted to using a broader range of competitiveness indicators – comparing prices with Tunisia's trading partners – to guide exchange rate policy. The rate of exchange is fixed by BCT according to the change in parities of a basket of currencies. Tunisia's flexible approach to exchange rate management has proved effective and the country was able to avoid excessive real appreciation of the dinar against an uncertain euro, and a consequent loss of competitiveness in the European market.

The dinar remained almost stable against the euro from January to 24 August 2000, during which time it depreciated by 10.7 per cent against the US dollar, by 5.5 per cent against the yen and by 2.5 per cent against sterling. In terms of annual drift in the year to July 2000, the value of the dinar fell by 18.78 per cent against the yen, by 9.94 per cent against the US dollar, by 5.66 per cent against the Moroccan dirham and by 5.80 per cent against sterling. Over the same period the dinar depreciated by just 0.9 per cent against the euro.

Since the introduction of the single European currency in 1999, exchange transactions on the interbank market have been negotiated in euros, replacing those currencies now absorbed in the euro zone. This change did not however alter the basis of exchange rate policy affecting the dinar.

This pragmatic approach illustrates the authorities' ability to react and adapt rapidly to economic policy challenges, an important asset in Tunisia's successful economic management. The government, however, continues its policy of not allowing the dinar to be traded on international markets. Government exchange controls for Tunisians travelling abroad were recently relaxed to allow them to take up to TD1,000 a year out of the country, double the previous limit of TD500 a year.

The economic role of government departments and agencies

Several government departments and agencies play leading roles in shaping and implementing Tunisia's economic policies. The key ministries are outlined below.

The Finance Ministry (Ministère des Finances)

This develops and implements state policy concerning financial, monetary and fiscal matters. Within this framework it participates in the setting of economic objectives and the design of appropriate mechanisms for realising policies.

The ministry's wide-ranging remit includes administration of the state budget, control over revenue and capital flows, management of customs and other duties, responsibility for aspects of financial legislation and regulations, treasury management, organisation and management of public finances. It also works with other ministries to implement policies where government finance is involved, such as the dispensation of state aid to enterprises.

The ministry is also charged with preparing and establishing government policy on credit. In this respect, it ultimately supervises banks and financial institutions, including insurance companies and mutual societies. It works closely with BCT to control the government's monetary supply, interest rates, and exchange controls, as well as functioning as a clearing house for the banking sector.

The Ministry of Economic Development (Ministère du Développement Economique)

This plays an important role in shaping Tunisia's economy by working with other departments and agencies to coordinate the government's national, regional and sector-specific policies for economic development. The ministry has a significant input in Tunisia's budget preparation and is also responsible for policies for restructuring public enterprises and services as well as privatisation.

The Ministry of International Co-operation and Foreign Investment (Ministère de la Coopération Internationale et de l'Investissement Extérieur)

This works closely with the Economic Development Ministry in determining and implementing strategies for attracting foreign investment to Tunisia. Under its auspices, the Agency for the Promotion of Industry (API – Agence de Promotion de l'Industrie) was set up to encourage and facilitate foreign investment. The Ministry of International Co-operation and Foreign Investment is charged with the decision of awarding incentives to investors and along with BCT, issuing import licences. These are discussed in subsequent chapters.

According to International Co-operation and Foreign Investment Minister Fethi Merdassi:

> The ministry's role is to co-ordinate Tunisia's investment effort, to make these developments as quickly as possible, but only after concerted study. We still have a rather fragile economy and, therefore, need to go in phases – and we need the Europeans, our biggest investors, to come with us.

The ministry is very active in the Euro-Med process. As Merdassi observes:

> Euro-Med means companies coming into Tunisia to export back into the European market. Eighty per cent of European companies come here saying they are looking to improve their production costs.

The ministry, API and the Foreign Investment Promotion Agency (FIPA) have produced an impressive body of studies and incentives to make this process happen.

Economic liberalisation and privatisation

Economic reforms over the past decade have created a progressively more liberal environment which is favourable to private initiative and enterprise growth. Reforms have included more liberal price, trade and exchange regimes and have moved Tunisia towards adopting a market system as the basis of economic organisation, management and policymaking.

Price liberalisation has allowed the market progressively more influence in determining industrial and consumer prices, although subsidies remain in certain areas, notably in some foodstuffs and petroleum. Prices have also been increasingly driven by the loosening of foreign trade restrictions, which has consequently subjected domestic markets to price pressure from international competitors. Around 87 per cent of producer prices are now market driven and 96 per cent of production is subject to international competition.

Foreign and domestic investments freely flow into several vibrant sectors of the economy. These investments stimulate enterprise growth and consequently improve living standards amongst Tunisians, hence creating greater capital mobility and larger domestic markets for goods and services bought by businesses and consumers.

Liberalisation has also increased the availability of foreign financing resulting in a shift from domestic to foreign financing. In addition, domestic financing has come to rely more heavily on non-bank financing, a consequence of which has been a steady reduction in central government indebtedness to the domestic banking system.

The sum of these factors makes Tunisia an even more attractive location for business, hence stimulating more investments that bring not only greater capital flows, but also new technologies and valuable transfers of technical and management know-how. However,t while economic liberalisation stimulates economic growth, it also creates serious challenges. One is for Tunisia itself, as a nation competing with other countries for trade and investment. Another is faced by domestic businesses that face increased competition not only from overseas companies but also from foreign competitors locating in Tunisia's favourable environment for business.

The challenges and opportunities of liberalisation are seen most clearly in Tunisia's responses to its moves closer to Europe and in particularly in its Association Agreement with the European Union that will lead to the free exchange of industrial goods by 2008. The challenge for domestic businesses is that they must compete on equal terms with competitors in a free trade area. The government-supported *mise à niveau* (upgrading) programmes are levering standards of manufacturing and quality control up to levels competitive with European companies.

The opportunity for Tunisia is that it can compete on equal terms with other nations across the free trade environment. For example, lower production costs coupled with manufacturing and quality standards at a European level provide businesses operating in Tunisia with a national competitive advantage. Hence Tunisia is an operating location for dozens of foreign-owned first and second-tier automotive component manufacturers supplying parts to most of the major French, German and Swedish vehicle manufacturers.

Liberalisation is not a smooth process. Plans to open up areas of the economy to private initiative have faltered or suffered delays. The state still directly intervenes in commercial activities such as banking and telecommunications, which may also deter investment and private sector initiative from these sectors and make financing of schemes such as large-scale infrastructure projects less attractive. Deregulation has begun at the edges of some areas, for example electricity production and port handling facilities.

The process of liberalising external finances has yet to be completed. The dinar became convertible in 1992 and President Ben Ali has suggested it will be further deregulated. He stated during electioneering in 1999 that 'progress towards finalising the deregulation of the dinar' was possible as Tunisia had shown its ability to 'balance the finances of the nation's economy.'

An acceleration of deregulation and liberalisation processes, including the simplification of administrative and regulatory regimes, would help to realise these potential gains. Acceleration of the privatisation programme would release some very under-exploited state assets.

Outlook for privatisation

Even though the sale of major state assets may not have proceeded as quickly as some donors and the financial community might like, privatisation of public enterprises is a core dimension in Tunisia's framework for economic liberalisation. It fits the authorities' aim of integrating national activity in the global economy by opening up new opportunities for private sector initiatives, mobilising foreign investment and creating a dynamic financial market. According to Economic Development Minister Abdellatif Saddam:

> Privatisation in Tunisia has never been a question of budgets. We have undertaken privatisation for two reasons: firstly, to save employment by bringing capital, know-how and efficient practices into some previously badly managed state enterprises; and, secondly, to give local companies new perspectives. We started the process by divesting bad companies to give them new life, which also did have the affect of saving the state money. In a poorly functioning corporate state sector, there have been over 100 privatisations and the need only for 31 liquidations. Now the terrain has been established we have gone on to bigger divestments – notably of the cement works, a privatisation which would have been inconceivable before the years of steadily selling smaller concerns.

From an economic standpoint, the country's model for achieving sustainable growth through a process of steady reform is delivering tangible results

Tunisia has taken a gradualist approach to privatisation. State-owned enterprises with relatively few employees in non-strategic sectors, such as cement and milk, have been privatised. For now, the state retains a grip on its phosphate mines and the telecommunications, railways, airline and electricity distribution sectors. The

Exhibit 3.13
Privatisations 1987–mid 2000

	1987–91	*1992–96*	*1997– July 2000*	*Total 1987–2000*
Proceeds (TD million)	126	191	1,023	1,340
Enterprises concerned *	37	45	54	136
Number of operations	68	84	142	294

* Enterprises whose operations have been privatised in two or more stages appear in this table in the period during which the first operation was privatised.

Source: Ministry of Economic Development.

authorities' response to those who say they have not opened certain state-run sectors up more to the private sector is clear. The state will keep control over certain strategic industries, but private sector participation is to be encouraged in new activities. In respect of transport, water and energy utilities, this means a probable increase in state-owned companies extending concessions to the private sector.

Similarly, in sectors sometimes thought to be reserved solely for the state, such as phosphates, private operators are encouraged in new activities. A joint Tunisian-Canadian phosphates privately operated venture is already under way near Kef, but state-owned La Compagnie des Phosphates de Gafsa (CPG) will not in the foreseeable future be divesting its existing assets.

Privatisations involving 48 firms in the tourism, food, construction, trading and transport sectors netted the Treasury around TD190 million in the first seven years of the programme to 1994. The privatisation process picked up speed in 1995 with the sale of about 90 state-owned companies for more than TD1 billion, 70 per cent of which came from foreign investors. Four of the 90 companies privatised were cement plants which were sold for TD770 million. Privatisation receipts totalled TD1.34 billion at end-2000 from sales of state assets involving 136 enterprises in privatisation and restructuring (see Exhibit 3.13). Of these enterprises, 66 have been wholly privatised, 27 have been partially privatised, 31 have been liquidated and 12 other operations have

Sustained growth and much improved living conditions for most Tunisians have resulted in some observers citing Tunisia as a model of economic management for developing countries

received capital injections. According to Saddam, speaking to the authors of this book in December 2000:

> Privatisation has brought in TD1.4bn – around $1 billion at current value – and of this some two-thirds has come from abroad. In the cement works, our new foreign partners are investing, giving a clear sign of the value privatisation can bring. It shows that our operations have a real value, and that private management can create jobs.

While earlier privatisations failed to attract significant amounts of foreign capital, investment in all privatisations to July 2000 has been 67 per cent provided by foreign investors and 33 per cent by domestic investors. Official assessments of the sell-offs to date have shown that privatised firms had increased turnover by 35 per cent annually, created new jobs and added investment of about TD115 million.

The government has drawn boundaries around the privatisation process. Preservation of jobs and labour rights are essential elements of the privatisation process, which is limited to enterprises in competitive sectors. Business development and improved competitiveness should result from privatisation.

Decisions on privatisation are considered at the highest level by La Commission d'Assainissement et de Restructuration des Entreprises à Participations Publiques (CAREPP), presided over by the prime minister.

Financial institutions, notably the IMF, have urged Tunisia to quicken the pace of privatisation and its 2001 programme appears to commit the authorities to accelerating the process. The largest sell-off to date could net the Treasury up to TD1.847 billion from sales of state-assets in 41 enterprises operating in various fields.

Manufacturing companies dominate the list of firms to be privatised, which also includes several property companies and hotels and the country's oldest insurer Lloyd Tunisien. The privatisation of Lloyd, which has assets of TD3 million, will be the first privatisation in the insurance sector since Tunisia launched its programme.

Privatisation schedule for 2001

Hotels, health and spas

- Le Grand Hôtel Kerkennah;
- Hôtel Sufetela;
- Hôtel Julius El Jem;
- Hôtel Yasmina Hammamet;
- Hôtel Sahara Palace;
- Hôtel Molka;
- Hôtel Naur El ayn, Ain Draham;
- Hôtel les Sources Korbous;

- Station Thermale Hammam Bourguiba;
- Polyclinique Ettaoufik.

Other services

- Autotractor;
- Etablissements Louis Montenav;
- Société immobiliere de Gabès;
- Tunis center;
- Société de promotion economique de Bizerte;
- Société Nationale Immobilière Tunisienne (SNIT) – Nord;
- SNIT-Centre;
- SNIT-Sud.

Financial services

- L'Union Internationale des Banques;
- Lloyd Tunisien.

Agriculture and agribusiness

- Société de Developpement Agricole et de Dattes (SODAD);
- Société Tunisienne d'Aviculture (SOTAVI);
- Société Tunisienne du Sucre;
- Complexe Sucrier de Tunisie;
- Société Tunisienne de l'Industrie du Lait (STIL);

Mechanical and electromechanical industries

- Société Tunisienne de Trefilage (MAKI.ADA);
- Société Anonyme de Construction Electromecanique (SACEM);
- Société des Fonderies et de Mecaniques (SOFOMECA);
- Les Ateliers Mecaniques du Sahel (AMS);
- Société Tunisienne de Construction Mecanique et Navale (SOCOMENA);
- Société Agricultor Industrielle (SAGRI);
- Ateliers de Constructions Metalliques et de Maintenance de Gabès.

Other industries

- Société Tunisienne de Chaux;
- El Kanaouet S.A.;
- Union Generale de Jammal;
- Manufacture Tunisienne de Céramique;
- Les Platres Tunisiens;
- La Société Nationale de Liège;
- Complexe de Plastique de Mazzouna;

- Skanès Meubles;
- Société les Panneaux Normalises de la Foret de Tabarka.

The authorities have shied away from publishing ambitious privatisation schedules in the past, and were consequently criticised for a lack of transparency in their plans for privatisation. However, the problems in drawing up concrete plans were made clear when one of the slated sales faltered weeks after the 2001 privatisation schedule was revealed. Privatisation of state-owned bank Union Internationale de Banque (UIB) was set to take place after it had merged with Banque de Tunisie et des Emirates d'Investissement (BTEI). Unfortunately, the banks failed to complete their merger, which was expected by early 2001.

4 *Trade and export: engines of growth*

Policies for trade

Since at least the Phoenician epoch, Tunisians have had a vocation to trade. There was something of a historical symmetry about the restructuring of Tunisia's economy, as planned in the later 1980s and early 1990s, which focused on policies for trade liberalisation which were firmly rooted in the authorities' determination to grow an economy that integrates with the global economy. Unlike many other countries that embarked on structural adjustment, a trade liberalisation focus – tied into the encouragement of foreign investment to again make Tunisia a crossroads for international business – came naturally to Tunisians. As former Investment Minister Salah Brik Hannachi often pointed out, trans-Mediterranean trade, telecommunications and other routes which form the framework for a 21st century economy

Export orientation at the highest level

The Conseil Supérieur de l'Exportation et de l'Investissement (CSEI – High Council for Export and Investment) was created in 1997 at the start of the 9th Plan. The council's main tasks are to set objectives, draw up sectorial strategies, and evaluate and monitor the results of export activity. The CSEI meets when convened by the president every six months and whenever else necessary.

Under the chairmanship of the President of the Republic, the mix of ministries represented on the council reveals the key roles played by several departments, all of which must integrate their activities to produce effective strategies for export promotion. The CSEI comprises the prime minister as well as the ministers of foreign affairs, tourism and crafts, agriculture, trade, industry, economic development, higher education, vocational training and employment, communication technology, international cooperation and foreign investment, commerce, finance, transport and the Treasury.

Also on the council are the central bank governor, the president of l'Union Tunisienne de l'Industrie, du Commerce et de l'Artisanat (UTICA – Union of Industry, Commerce and Crafts), the secretary general of the Union Générale Tunisienne du Travail (UGTT – Tunisia's General Labour Union) and the president of the Union Tunisienne de l'Agriculture et de la Pêche (UTAP – Union of Agriculture and Fisheries).

in the Mediterranean Basin and its vast hinterland follow remarkably closely the communications networks built by the Romans.

However, while Tunisia has a vocation for trade, and has liberalised to provide a framework that develops local industry and encourages export-oriented foreign investment, the country has not opened up without taking other issues into account. The government also aims to create sustained economic and social development to promote jobs, living standards and other benefits that will reinforce political and social stability. To realise its global and national ambitions, policies broadly aim to create competitive advantage for Tunisia as a location for investment and commercial development, and prepare its stock of enterprises to defend national, and conquer international, markets.

Tunisia subscribed very early on to the notion that entry to world markets requires membership to clubs of countries that abide by free market rules in which trade must go, almost entirely unfettered by the state, in a liberal and competitive environment. The country is therefore a member of the World Trade Organisation (WTO), and in 1995 Tunisia become the first southern Mediterranean country to sign an Association Agreement with the European Union (AAEU). It is also a signatory to several more bilateral and regional free trade agreements.

The essential challenge has been to introduce and embed free market systems in a nation that until little more than 10 years ago had a very interventionist government, system and culture. Indeed, the state still plays a leading role in many areas of Tunisian life, but it has overseen a gradual opening, which now means that the market is relatively open.

The corollary of this situation is that Tunisia also has a population of individuals and businesses that expected, and sometimes still expect, state intervention in economic activity.

Even for a government dedicated to accelerated liberalisation a radical policy redirection takes time. Critics, including officials in some multilateral institutions and western governments, have said Tunisia's progress in liberalising trade has been slow. However, changing the culture and approach of a nation is arguably more difficult than changing its laws and is not achieved easily. Tunisia has adopted a gradualist and pragmatic approach to the task of freeing up its trading environment by introducing progressive and targeted reforms and measures.

A gradual opening bears fruit

Specific policies to free up trade have included the progressive reduction of tariffs, removal of price subsidies, dismantling of non-tariff barriers, overhaul of the fiscal system, privatisation and less state interference in competitive sectors.

Trade liberalisation has had a positive impact on investment. This required a lowering of barriers to entry by foreign investors and operators, but it has also required a gradual opening up of the domestic market. The net result is that Tunisia has become more competitive in international markets, but its domestic businesses face more competition in Tunisian and regional markets.

An important strand in Tunisia's policies for trade has, therefore, been to improve the competitiveness within its enterprise stock. Improving the competitiveness of both domestic and foreign commercial operations in Tunisia has also required overhauls and reforms to its transport, telecommunications and financial infrastructures as well as access to national and international distribution channels.

Exports are a key focus of trade development policies. The establishment of the Conseil Supérieur de l'Exportation et de l'Investissement (CSEI) chaired by the president underscores the importance accorded to export and related policies.

Trade barriers and tariffs

Tunisia has progressively dismantled barriers to trade, and is working with the European Union and WTO to iron out any inconsistencies in the trade regime. In excess of 95 per cent of imports do not now need prior licensing, compared with 1986 when only 23.6 per cent of imports could be freely imported. This has liberalised key sectors such as textiles in line with Tunisia's WTO commitments.

Tariffs and other taxes remain, particularly on consumer goods that compete with locally produced equivalents in key industries, such as textiles, and items that may adversely affect the economy. Certain luxury items attract a consumption tax of between 10 per cent and 500 per cent. Agricultural products frequently attract high import duties too. VAT is calculated on the base price of the goods plus any import duties, surcharges, and consumption taxes.

In specific sectors, imports are prohibited or actively disadvantaged. In October 1998, the authorities prohibited the import of certain agricultural products, including henna and some dates, claiming plant health reasons. Other agricultural products carry high import duties.

Certain imported products, including weapons or security-related materials and healthcare products, remain strictly controlled and are considered under specific rules to ensure state security.

Barriers for exports are understandably lower than those for imports. Export controls exist on some limited products. Prior authorisation is required for certain items, including those related to security, public order, hygiene, health, morality, protection of flora and fauna, and cultural heritage. Prior authorisation is required for export of goods in these areas. Other products may be required to meet international standards, or those of the importing country. Tunisia is progressively embracing ISO 9000 and European standards.

Physical trade and exports: current flows and future trends

Tunisia has a regular trade deficit, which according to official figures shown in Exhibits 4.1 and 4.2 widened during the first eight months of 2000. Pressure on the trade deficit was due to higher imports, particularly of cereals to make up for low domestic output depressed by severe drought conditions. By November, imports in 2000 had increased over the first 11 months of 1999 by around 17.2 per cent to TD10.76 billion.

There is now an established trend of rising exports in the pattern of Tunisia's trade. The value of exports during 2000 was boosted by sharp increases in goods exports and strong prices for petroleum products sold abroad.

Exhibit 4.1
Trade balance, 1995–99

	1995	*1996*	*1997*	*1998*	*1999*
Quantity (tonnes '000s)					
Imports	12,385.1	11,312.6	11,777.7	11,755.3	13,068.4
Exports	11,232.5	11,890.3	10,779.9	10,417.5	10,179.0
Value (TD million)					
Imports	7,464.1	7,498.8	8,793.5	9,489.5	10,070.5
Exports	5,172.9	5,372.0	6,147.9	6,518.3	6,966.9
Balance	-2,291.2	-2,126.8	-2,645.6	-2,971.2	-3,103.6
Import cover (%)	69.30	71.63	69.91	68.68	69.18

Source: Institut National de la Statistique.

Exhibit 4.2
Trade balance, Jan–Aug 1999 to Jan–Aug 2000

1999	*Jan*	*Feb*	*Mar*	*Apr*	*May*	*Jun*	*Jul*	*Aug*
Quantity (tonnes '000s)								
Imports	869.4	1,892.9	2,863.0	3,994.6	5,039.5	5,967.4	6,918.9	7,932.7
Exports	870.2	1,614.5	2,671.3	3,358.7	4,026.2	4,787.5	5,596.1	6,578.4
Value (TD million)								
Imports	643.2	1,374.0	2,190.7	3,104.6	3,941.2	4,851.5	5,864.7	6,533.4
Exports	486.0	1,074.0	1,700.1	2,259.3	2,798.7	3,358.4	4,000.5	4,474.7
Balance	-157.2	-300.0	-490.6	-845.3	-1,142.5	-1,493.1	-1,864.2	-2,058.7
Import cover (%)	75.55	78.16	77.60	72.77	71.01	69.22	68.21	68.48
2000	*Jan*	*Feb*	*Mar*	*Apr*	*May*	*Jun*	*Jul*	*Aug*
Quantity (tonnes '000s)								
Imports	1,213.4	2,284.9	3,531.1	4,629.2	5,829.8	6,832.9	7,751.6	8,906.9
Exports	850.0	1,784.8	2,949.9	3,763.5	4,374.7	5,058.5	6,050.3	6,846.8
Value (TD million)								
Imports	856.1	1,769.4	2,671.7	3,800.9	4,949.3	5,869.2	6,780.0	7,728.3
Exports	621.5	1,306.2	1,990.6	2,658.4	3,393.4	3,952.8	4,683.8	5,214.9
Balance	-234.6	-463.2	-681.1	-1,142.5	-1,555.9	-1,916.4	-2,096.2	-2,513.4
Import cover (%)	72.59	73.82	74.50	69.94	68.56	67.34	69.08	67.47

Source: Institut National de la Statistique.

The government has said it expects exports of goods and services to increase by 8.9 per cent in 2001 against a projected 8.5 per cent rise of imports. This would keep the current account deficit within the limit of 3 per cent of the GDP.

Statistics published by the central bank highlight the unique trends in Tunisia's trade over the first seven months of 2000, but also point to clear growth in the volumes of import and export trades and the consequences of this growth on the economy (see Exhibit 4.3)

An important role for tourism

Exhibit 4.3 also notes the important role of tourism in the trading economy. Earnings from tourism account for 18.6 per cent of Tunisia's exports and the sector is instrumental

Exhibit 4.3

Main trade indicators (TD million unless otherwise indicated)

	First seven months			*Variations in %*	
	1998	*1999*	*2000*	*1999/98*	*1999/2000*
Investment projects[1]					
Agriculture and fishing[2]	165.3	179.3	207.2	8.5	15.6
Manufacturing industries	644.3	694.3	788.8	7.8	13.6
Services (other than tourism)	163.3	151.4	237.5	-7.3	56.9
Tourism	156.4	288.8	236.7	84.7	-18.0
High and medium voltage electricity consumption (kWh million)[1]	1,948.5	2,074.0	2,264.1	6.4	9.2
of which: by the industrial sector[1]	1,280.4	1,346.3	1,473.6	5.1	9.5
Balance of trade					
Overall exports FOB	3,769.8	4,000.4	4,683.8	6.1	17.1
Overall imports CIF	5,523.3	5,864.7	6,780.0	6.2	15.6
Trade deficit excluding foodstuffs[3]	1,532.0	1,854.9	2,036.2	322.9	181.3
Overall trade deficit[3]	1,753.5	1,864.3	2,096.2	110.8	231.9
Overall coverage rate (%)	68.3	68.2	69.1	-0.1 point	0.9 point
Increase in consumer prices					
Rise since the beginning of the year (%)	0.7	0.7	1.1		
In terms of monthly averages (%)	3.3	2.8	3.1		
Tourism					
Non-residents' inflows (1,000 individuals)	2,468	2,671	2,745	8.2	2.8
Overall bed-nights (1,000 units)	16,064	18,819	19,256	17.2	2.3
Non-residents' bed-nights (1,000 units)[4]	8,798	10,004	10,380	13.7	3.8

[1] End-June of each year.

[2] Including integrated agro-food projects.

[3] Variations expressed in millions of dinars.

[4] End-May of each year.

Source: Banque Centrale de Tunisie, August 2000.

in offsetting the trade deficit. Remittances from Tunisians working abroad also help in this respect.

Tourism was Tunisia's highest net earner of foreign exchange in 1999, and has been an increasingly important source of employment. During the 1990s, income from tourism more than doubled while the number of visitors has nearly tripled. With many new hotels under construction, and planning permits for more, capacity has grown fast over the past few years. Significantly, levels of investment in the tourism sector fell by 18 per cent in the first seven months of 2000, suggesting the Tunisian tourism sector is close to capacity.

Export trends

Textiles, clothing and leather represented 32.4 per cent of Tunisia's exports in 1999. In the same year, mechanical and electrical goods accounted for 10.7 per cent and the chemical industries 7.9 per cent of all exports. Including an 8.4 per cent contribution to exports from other industries, the entire manufacturing sector produced 59.4 per cent of all exports in 1999. Phosphates, their by-products and other minerals, cement, as well as crude and refined petroleum products are also major exports.

The value of textile exports, which doubled between 1991 and 1996, slowed down significantly in 1999 (see Exhibits 4.4 and 4.5). Earnings from foreign sales of textiles in 1999 amounted to little more than 2 per cent more than the value of export sales in 1998. However,

Exhibit 4.4

Principal exports, 1995–99 (TD '000s)

	1995	*1996*	*1997*	*1998*	*1999*
Petroleum and derivatives	436,900	563,028	555,879	417,722	497,952
Textiles	2,347,200	2,484,300	2,683,500	2,949,282	3,013,120
Olive oil	216,613	117,096	288,450	213,300	382,741
Phosphates and other minerals	40,146	44,405	52,053	45,535	48,707
Fertilisers	281,641	318,731	309,259	344,978	347,317
Chemicals	256,543	298,717	369,376	376,843	376,375
Market produce	72,075	58,525	60,278	82,238	66,618
Sugar and sweets	2,653	3,269	4,941	4,661	4,953
Leather and footwear	231,911	258,206	305,132	329,632	373,489
Fish and shellfish	74,073	90,845	107,365	125,751	102,073
Vegetables and flowers	4,803	7,799	5,015	5,883	8,531
Lead	176	450	400	804	142
Machinery and electrical equipment	367,254	415,567	537,547	692,500	668,900
Beverages	18,135	16,902	27,608	22,227	25,255
Packaging and materials	36,679	32,984	38,913	39,584	53,919

Source: Institut National de la Statistique.

Exhibit 4.5
Principal exports, Jan–Aug 1999 to Jan–Aug 2000 (TD '000s)

1999	*Jan*	*Feb*	*Mar*	*Apr*	*May*	*Jun*	*Jul*	*Aug*
Petroleum and derivatives	35,967	49,096	87,100	104,000	132,400	175,601	207,600	261,788
Textiles	232,973	506,424	765,510	1,023,935	1,251,760	1,529,903	1,849,384	2,004,136
Olive oil	21,634	41,669	118,954	149,448	189,517	198,514	216,344	276,254
Phosphates and other minerals	3,739	8,787	12,975	18,382	22,550	28,308	29,754	34,016
Fertilisers	17,782	50,629	91,365	110,830	117,409	134,895	161,616	195,261
Chemicals	25,585	54,039	87,079	120,673	154,908	177,045	208,339	243,775
Market produce	9,903	15,113	18,447	20,975	22,879	24,005	24,855	25,513
Sugar and sweets	256	889	1,567	2,011	2,428	2,604	2,817	3,100
Leather and footwear	26,911	58,316	89,726	120,894	153,292	182,959	219,058	235,139
Fish and shellfish	5,164	11,280	18,933	29,377	42,117	52,333	62,346	66,188
Vegetables and flowers	1,153	2,757	4,351	5,713	6,516	6,812	7,213	7,467
Lead	4	37	79	79	79	100	100	100
Machinery and electrical equipment	50,852	115,342	180,273	245,354	310,279	375,131	440,563	477,495
Beverages	917	5,088	8,076	9,646	12,213	15,357	16,410	17,760
Packaging and materials	2,644	7,224	11,933	16,236	21,276	26,264	30,491	34,055
2000	*Jan*	*Feb*	*Mar*	*Apr*	*May*	*Jun*	*Jul*	*Aug*
Petroleum and derivatives	60,836	128,000	244,500	296,900	359,000	414,943	495,777	547,806
Textiles	272,024	556,969	823,074	1,125,947	1,403,937	1,707,963	2,017,861	2,224,940
Olive oil	35,024	78,283	106,868	120,928	140,979	156,308	182,112	199,180
Phosphates and other minerals	6,585	10,873	16,690	21,955	25,147	28,432	35,627	38,871
Fertilisers	20,239	59,852	91,742	121,969	123,186	144,464	191,782	244,619
Chemicals	32,838	70,085	101,138	129,106	154,994	184,937	215,036	237,559
Market produce	12,001	18,352	21,483	25,166	28,893	30,135	31,213	32,370
Sugar and sweets	114	246	677	974	1,249	1,477	1,703	2,009
Leather and footwear	29,988	71,756	108,121	146,779	189,284	223,921	263,350	294,034
Fish and shellfish	3,920	9,652	18,093	27,279	46,229	57,698	69,146	74,169
Vegetables and flowers	666	1,723	3,296	4,594	5,156	5,494	5,940	6,347
Lead	–	–	–	–	5	10	15	20
Machinery and electrical equipment	64,973	143,575	217,585	307,090	395,716	469,547	551,342	604,730
Beverages	2,486	3,481	5,192	8,208	12,521	14,007	14,742	16,960
Packaging and materials	4,670	9,612	14,362	19,335	24,238	28,965	33,328	40,333

Source: Institut National de la Statistique.

with improved productivity and a new focus on selling higher value goods abroad, growth in the first eight months of 2000 is stronger, with the value of exports amounting to TD2.26 million compared with TD 2.00 million in the period January to August 1999.

Agriculture no longer dominates the Tunisian economy but it is still important in the export mix with food products accounting for around 10 per cent of exports. Dates and olive oil are the country's most visible exports on world markets. Market produce, flowers, vegetables and seafood are also exported. A diversifying food processing industry is producing an increasing volume of added-value food products for export.

A structural flaw in several key segments of Tunisia's export sector, including textiles, is a reliance on subcontracting from European principals without any real partnership between Tunisian and foreign investors. The central bank recommends an export strategy refocused on actions to create a lasting and sustainable growth in the export of goods and services. This could be achieved through mergers across all sectors, either among Tunisian companies or with foreign companies. Such an approach would work particularly well in the agricultural and food-processing sectors which has the potential to create more added-value products at competitive prices.

Import trends

About one-third of Tunisia's imports are mechanical and electrical goods and around one-quarter of imports are textiles and leather (see Exhibits 4.6 and 4.7). Crude and refined petroleum products represent about 8 per cent of imports. Iron and steel combined accounts for 7 per cent of imports, as do food products.

Exhibit 4.6

Principal imports, 1995–99 (TD '000s)

	1995	*1996*	*1997*	*1998*	*1999*
Dairy products	50,590	27,900	42,534	24,840	21,239
Coffee, tea and spices	38,241	35,129	47,950	47,998	42,859
Cereals	402,900	256,000	346,800	317,500	265,876
Sugar and sweets	68,662	87,437	92,188	108,278	85,278
Natural gas	145,000	106,700	58,200	32,500	56,400
Petrol derivatives	354,600	469,600	588,000	411,500	561,300
Pharmaceuticals	136,064	140,654	164,113	168,819	183,175
Plastics	267,693	256,869	295,147	340,320	343,725
Vegetable oils	111,011	112,574	99,610	140,200	126,732
Sulphur	95,055	78,439	92,923	71,774	67,581
Wood and wood products	121,435	99,331	134,573	127,761	125,814
Textiles	1,746,864	1,836,621	2,029,131	2,335,821	2,286,900
Cast iron and steel	363,053	340,186	369,408	462,341	435,485
Mechanical machinery and engines	864,302	956,938	1,089,300	1,298,303	1,314,983
Electrical machinery and apparatus	516,131	596,400	710,303	845,760	847,577
Vehicles, cycles and tractors	446,378	494,237	611,732	627,800	776,399
Optical and scientific equipment	144,226	143,944	157,648	169,283	191,943

Source: Institut National de la Statistique.

Exhibit 4.7

Principal imports, Jan–Aug 1999 to Jan–Aug 2000 (TD '000s)

1999	*Jan*	*Feb*	*Mar*	*Apr*	*May*	*Jun*	*Jul*	*Aug*
Dairy products	755	2,189	4,152	6,048	7,589	9,605	11,827	13,568
Coffee, tea and spices	2,269	7,917	14,468	18,928	21,555	22,377	24,691	26,456
Cereals	20,500	74,700	95,200	109,931	135,622	148,732	166,737	187,146
Sugar and sweets	932	7,914	17,840	31,622	37,577	41,706	42,388	46,199
Natural gas	100	..	8,800	8,800	8,900	23,100	23,200	23,300
Petrol derivatives	20,000	65,800	85,800	100,900	141,000	174,200	197,900	248,700
Pharmaceuticals	10,846	21,051	38,187	53,139	68,197	85,864	102,441	121,583
Plastics	23,454	49,451	60,139	112,493	143,154	171,506	200,905	225,157
Vegetable oils	11,758	20,135	39,558	44,919	56,139	75,141	80,521	89,305
Sulphur	5,245	8,702	14,400	19,750	26,270	28,632	39,345	43,844
Wood and wood products	13,265	22,838	32,991	46,883	62,487	71,111	80,982	92,341
Textiles	147,114	340,304	520,162	731,016	940,754	1,165,349	1,365,801	1,485,633
Cast iron and steel	25,076	63,304	106,217	144,759	177,219	210,311	242,386	266,600
Mechanical machinery and engines	101,797	203,156	301,332	413,454	542,303	666,739	782,569	884,004
Electrical machinery and apparatus	59,380	125,124	197,236	268,071	344,203	419,960	488,256	543,980
Vehicles, cycles and tractors	58,068	111,673	168,253	225,693	288,519	357,783	436,174	528,839
Optical and scientific equipment	15,414	29,554	44,920	60,275	77,299	93,902	109,983	121,546

2000	*Jan*	*Feb*	*Mar*	*Apr*	*May*	*Jun*	*Jul*	*Aug*
Dairy products	2,521	3,788	6,307	9,155	9,922	12,304	13,621	16,975
Coffee, tea and spices	3,059	4,361	6,720	12,025	17,150	23,485	26,653	30,985
Cereals	15,412	51,377	74,136	100,944	135,196	164,430	195,262	216,995
Sugar and sweets	2,826	18,469	24,102	34,166	41,907	42,170	43,088	48,025
Natural gas	..	..	..	..	..	..	..	..
Petrol derivatives	94,300	130,868	275,700	355,800	432,000	499,100	553,100	668,064
Pharmaceuticals	18,574	35,554	51,311	66,049	83,363	101,953	119,700	135,181
Plastics	32,700	65,740	104,902	145,317	182,730	222,857	258,265	293,928
Vegetable oils	11,675	21,927	31,647	38,192	48,367	54,710	68,039	83,634
Sulphur	11,935	18,499	26,840	32,742	42,905	51,886	58,125	64,274
Wood and wood products	9,467	19,602	29,137	44,632	59,806	71,573	88,096	104,163
Textiles	203,920	389,358	556,750	784,764	1,043,833	1,259,710	1,474,122	1,628,613
Cast iron and steel	25,568	65,377	116,527	153,106	206,013	249,121	278,621	317,521
Mechanical machinery and engines	107,337	223,349	343,225	488,999	622,106	751,851	871,986	1,025,731
Electrical machinery and apparatus	76,512	154,671	222,969	309,773	397,488	487,160	580,454	660,836
Vehicles, cycles and tractors	53,773	111,505	173,573	231,805	305,669	370,276	444,644	540,329
Optical and scientific equipment	26,091	46,443	63,469	83,350	104,307	122,260	139,703	159,488

Source: Institut National de la Statistique.

Despite steep rises in agricultural production since the 1970s, imports of food and feedstock have soared to meet 40 per cent of domestic requirements. In an address to the nation on the 13th anniversary of his accession to power, President Ben Ali noted Tunisia's performance in the agriculture and fisheries sector but emphasised that:

> Self-sufficiency is a strategic aim, and food security is part of the security and sovereignty of peoples. Therefore, we call today for the setting up of a solid national plan for strategic reserves of some basic agricultural products, in order to secure the country's needs, and to protect the interests of producers and consumers.

A national consultation process will discuss this plan.

Trade financing

Tunisia's good credit rating means that banks are keen to provide trade financing services, such as letter of credit confirmation, and export credit agencies (ECAs) are on cover for the full range of guarantees. Commercial banks provide short-term trade finance, providing businesses with loans in several structures. They also offer a range of cash, credit and exchange services to ensure domestic and international trade transactions.

Some specialist trade financiers are emerging, including two factoring companies. Tunisie Factoring and Unifactor purchase from clients trade receivables, which they collect.

Pre-export financing is available on preferential terms for certain goods and sectors. Typically, 30 per cent of anticipated exports in one year may be financed. Up to 80 per cent of intended date exports or 60 days of citrus fruits may be financed. Pre-export finance may also be available for a 100 per cent carry over of olive oil and wine stocks.

Buyers' loans – typically up to a maximum amount of 80 per cent of contract value – may be extended to importers via a domestic commercial bank by a foreign bank, thereby allowing the importer to pay the foreign supplier cash. Suppliers' loans may be extended to exporters offering payment terms to importing customers, typically up to a maximum amount of 100 per cent of the term payment.

Commercial banks can provide exchange risk cover to importers, exporters and service providers paying or being paid in foreign currency. Typically, cover extends to a maximum term of 12 months for credit purchases (imports), nine months for credit sales (exports) and 12 months for credit sales of services abroad.

Currency options to protect businesses negotiating foreign currency loans can be bought at a premium and guarantee the right to buy a currency at a rate and expiry date agreed in advance. These options are offered by commercial banks and insured by the central bank.

Credit is generally considered to be available from the country's banks, reflected in the significant proportion of short-term credit used in the economy (see Exhibit 4.8).

Exhibit 4.8
Short-term credits by economic activity, 1995–99 (TD)

	1995	*1996*	*1997*	*1998*	*1999*
Agriculture and fisheries	**461,989**	**463,225**	**511,975**	**531,768**	**550,947**
Industry	**3,317,346**	**3,597,629**	**3,807,812**	**3,981,708**	**4,158,848**
Mines	71,025	78,903	40,553	24,896	15,531
Energy	28,297	35,199	41,052	32,938	40,833
Manufacturing industries	2,838,464	3,049,609	3,257,197	3,446,703	3,598,363
Building and civil engineering	379,560	433,918	469,010	477,171	504,121
Services	**2,433,844**	**2,926,002**	**3,218,188**	**3,572,554**	**4,077,103**
Transport	122,032	147,248	178,748	205,730	214,277
Tourism	404,875	505,035	622,224	807,144	906,610
Commerce	1,355,787	1,517,249	1,606,116	1,634,668	1,903,138
Total credits	**6,213,179**	**6,986,856**	**7,537,975**	**8,086,030**	**8,786,898**

Source: Banque Centrale de Tunisie.

Trading partners

Over 82 per cent of Tunisia's exports in 1999 sold into European markets, the vast majority to EU member states. Four primary clients account for around 70 per cent of total exports. Tunisia's primary trading partner is France, which takes around 25 per cent of all exports. About 20 per cent go to Italy, some 15 per cent sell into Germany while Belgium and Luxembourg combined take about 7 per cent. Tunisia's main sources of imports are France (which provides around 25 per cent of imports), Italy (15 per cent), Germany (12.5 per cent) and Belgium/Luxembourg (7 per cent).

European exports to Tunisia amounted to €5.7 billion in 1999, while Tunisian exports to the EU amounted to €4.3 billion, resulting in a negative balance of €1.4 billion for Tunisia. Exports to Tunisia from the EU are expected to increase further as preferential trading arrangements for member state companies are now in place.

On aggregate, Tunisia has not gained market share in its main EU markets since 1994. In contrast to the emerging eastern and central European countries, it has not gained sufficient market share in textile products to offset the lower than average growth of this sector in the EU. Tunisia's overall market share of total EU imports is low – at a fraction of 1 per cent – and static compared with competing regions. Asian economies pushed their market share up from 4.6 per cent to 7.3 per cent during the 1990s when eastern and central European exporters to the EU tripled their market share to around 2.4 per cent.

As well as skewing production to higher value-added goods, Tunisia has taken a number of actions to improve export performance in Europe and in the global market place. Reforms include an overhaul of sea transport arrangements to quash the oligopoly struck between state-owned and foreign companies on the strategic Tunis-Marseille sea route, which led to a 10 per cent saving in transportation costs. Customs clearance procedures are being simplified with the introduction of the liasse unique (single document).

Association Agreement with the European Union

Tunisia's relations with the EU have been critical to developments in recent years. In 1995, Tunisia signed an Association Agreement with the EU (AAEU), which entered into force on 1 March 1998 and will lead to a Euro-Tunisian free trade area by the year 2008. The agreement prescribes a far-reaching liberalisation of trade relations, enhanced financial and technical cooperation and close collaboration and dialogue in several areas, including cultural and political matters.

Perspective

For the EU, the agreement with Tunisia is part of its strategy for deepening its relations with its southern neighbours, with the objective of building a Euro-Mediterranean free trade area. The AAEU is established under the auspices of the Euro-Mediterranean Partnership between the EU and its 12 Mediterranean partners. The partnership was established at the Conference of EU and Mediterranean Foreign Ministers in Barcelona (27-28 November 1995), hence the negotiations at bilateral and multilateral or regional levels between the partners is known as the Barcelona Process.

Apart from Tunisia, other countries with which AAEUs have been ratified and are in force are Israel, Morocco and Jordan. Negotiations with Egypt were being finalised as at January 2001, while those with Lebanon were advancing. The remaining partners are Syria, Algeria, the Palestinian Authority, Turkey, Cyprus and Malta. Libya currently has observer status at certain meetings.

The AAEU is the mechanism for implementing free trade across the Euro-Mediterranean area linking, supposedly by 2010, the 15 EU member states and the 12 Mediterranean partners. With EFTA and central and eastern European candidate countries for EU enlargement, at a later stage, a wider free trade zone could include around 40 states and up to 800 million consumers.

Implications for Tunisia

For Tunisia, the AAEU calls for full participation in a Euro-Mediterranean free trade area for industrial goods by 2008. This means that Tunisia will enjoy preferential access to European markets. In exchange it must dismantle all tariff and non-tariff barriers, a process that has a profound fiscal impact since prior to the agreement customs duties alone accounted for one-fifth of tax duties.

The cost of eliminating the revenues barred in the agreement is likely to have reached 3.5 per cent of GDP by 2008. Moreover, reduced tariffs leading to cheaper imported goods may stimulate consumer spending, hence widening the trade and external current account deficits.

Restrictions and tariffs on many goods have been abolished while for certain items, tariffs will be phased out over a 12-year period. Full trade liberalisation for agriculture is not anticipated in the agreement and tariffs may still apply to some agricultural goods.

The dismantling of customs duties has required Tunisia to make substantial reforms to its fiscal, economic and industrial structures. Adjustments in these areas are also required if Tunisia is to meet the tough conditions in the agreement which call for a seamless harmonisation of the regulatory environment across the free trade area.

Over 82 per cent of Tunisia's exports in 1999 sold into European markets

Practices liable to distort trade between the partners must be abolished. This calls for Tunisia to phase out price subsidies, monopolies, and preferential arrangements for state-owned enterprises.

Harmonisation of physical standards is also called for in areas such as transport and telecommunications as well as rules and regulations in areas such as accounting and financial services.

In the light of the tough demands of the AAEU, economic and financial cooperation has been strengthened and financially supported by the EU, mainly through the MEDA programme. Tunisia has also received support for reforms associated with the agreement from the IMF, particularly through technical assistance to help identify areas where tax measures can compensate from revenues lost from customs duties.

The AAEU calls for dialogue on social issues to identify priority areas for collaborative actions. The reduction of immigration into Europe is one such area and through regionally targeted development support for Tunisia, efforts are made to reintegrate illegal immigrants into their country of origin. Other prioritised cooperative actions have focused on the inclusion of women in society, improving educational standards and broadening social services provided, particularly to women and children.

Benefits and drawbacks

Tunisia expects long-term gains from the AAEU, placing it at the very centre of its economic development policy, to an extent unprecedented among the Mediterranean partners. A study by the International Co-operation and Foreign Investment Ministry estimated that the agreement would eventually yield a gain of 1.4 per cent of GDP when all factors of production are redeployed. In the short run, the ministry's study estimated negligible net gains.

The longer-term benefits for Tunisia under the agreement can be simplistically listed as a virtuous circle in which foreign direct investment leads to improved competitiveness, job creation and better productivity yielding profits, some of which return to become more investments. Achieving this flow however presupposes that Tunisia is able to reallocate factors of production to areas of the economy where economies of scale of European proportions can be established.

Productivity gains should be achievable as a result of Tunisia's serious efforts to raise the quality of industrial production. Business should also benefit from improved transport, telecommunications, financial and regulatory infrastructures.

Jobs will be created in areas where Tunisia maintains labour cost advantages, although whether more jobs are lost through consolidation, mergers, the utilisation of technologies or the elimination of enterprises by stronger foreign competition remains one of the most critical tests of the agreement.

Mise à niveau (upgrading)

Some of the greatest challenges in the AAEU are not faced by governments and large institutions but by companies, notably the southern Mediterranean partners' large stock of smaller, family run enterprises. Notwithstanding competitive disadvantages, such as poor infrastructure and high energy costs, these have been asked to compete against much larger and sophisticated European companies.

In this respect, the *mise à niveau* (upgrading) initiative is central to Tunisia's efforts to integrate its enterprise stock not only with Europe but also in the global economy. It has received support from the EU and the World Bank and aims to lever Tunisia's commercial enterprises to international standards. In the period 1996-2000, expenditure in the programme was estimated at US$2.5 billion.

The initiative essentially aims to improve competitiveness by instilling in businesses technologies, technical and managerial competencies and approaches to quality control consistent with Tunisia's desired position in the global economy. Of the 2,000 companies targeted by the Bureau de Mise à Niveau in 1996, around half had by mid-2000 introduced a modernisation and restructuring programme.

North African links

Tunisia has also sought to harmonise trade agreements with other partners, particularly with states in the Union du Maghreb Arabe (UMA – Union of Arab Maghreb States), in which Algeria, Libya, Mauritania and Morocco are also members. North Africa represents a potentially important market for Tunisian companies – and foreign companies based in Tunisia, the easiest operating environment (with the possible exception of Morocco). However, trade data show that trade within the UMA region remains very low – and is often dependent on the fortunes of bilateral political relations between Maghreb states.

Tunisia is especially favoured by companies looking for a route to sell into Libya. Tunisia's Zarzis free trade zone and facilities of Djerba help to facilitate this business. As at early 2001, the Libyan market was enjoying an upturn as international sanctions waned and high oil prices gave a major boost to the largely state-controlled economy; Tunisia was also enjoying a period of improved relations with Libya.

Other alliances

Tunisia also participates in the Arab Free Trade Agreement and has trading agreements with the United States, Canada, Japan, Switzerland and Australia. Free trade agreements have been agreed with Morocco, Egypt and Jordan. Tunisia is also a WTO member.

5 *The financial system and the banking sector: mobilisers of the economy*

Banque Centrale de Tunisie, a strong central bank

Tunisia's sustained growth is frequently attributed to the country's consistent policy framework. The central bank, through the financial system, influences the macroeconomic environment of this framework and through its regulatory and supervisory roles in the banking system, it also plays a vital role in shaping the financial supports in the microeconomic environments in which economic activities take place.

The main role of Banque Centrale de Tunisie (BCT – the central bank) is to protect the internal and the external value of the dinar and preserve its stability. It therefore controls monetary circulation and credit allocation by means of indirect instruments of monetary policy and oversees the smooth functioning of the financial and the banking system.

The BCT is responsible for issuing all Tunisian dinar coins and banknotes, dealing in foreign currencies, administering exchange control, and it acts as banker for the government and for banks. BCT also has the authority to define and monitor prudential regulation in the banking and financial sectors.

In terms of dealings with foreign exchange, BCT is responsible for safe keeping and managing the country's reserve in gold and in foreign currencies. In its role as an administrator of exchange controls, the bank oversees exchange rate stability and is responsible for implementing exchange regulation and legislation. It grants licences to financial intermediaries and guarantees that financial institutions comply with regulations.

As banker to the government, BCT is financial agent for all of the state's cash, banking and credit transactions. It raises, on the state's behalf, funds in foreign currencies. Details of its borrowing policy are examined in Chapter 3.

It keeps the Treasury current account at its Tunis head office and at its branches. All debit and credit transactions on this account are carried out free of charge. BCT has branches at Bizerte, Sousse, Sfax, Nabeul, Gabès, Gafsa, Kasserine, Kairouan, Medenine, Jendouba and Monastir.

In its role as banker to the banks, BCT may receive on interest-free account, sums paid mainly by banks and other bodies entitled to carry out credit transactions. Only deposits in foreign currencies earn interest.

Tunisia's central bank, Banque Centrale de Tunisie

Authority is exercised over the banking system by the central bank, which defines prudential regulation and exercises a control on banks and financial establishments. The main purpose of this control is to guarantee the safety of deposits and of the banking system and penalise disciplinary misconduct

Among its other tasks, BCT participates in the capital of Société Interbancaire de Télécompensation (SIBTEL – electronic-clearing interbank company). BCT also explores ways to mobilise external resources for the benefit of the state by identifying points of access to the capital market with the best conditions of cost and maturity. It assists private and public enterprises in arranging external borrowing operations and analysing financing offers.

The central bank also provides information services. It manages an information system to help banks appreciate their true value risks incurred on the basis of unpaid cheques, risks and balance sheets. BCT also collects and publishes economic information.

Ratings agencies keep in close contact

Communicating economic and banking sector information is important in terms of BCT's work with international rating agencies whose ratings affect access to financial markets. Ratings for Tunisia are shown in Exhibit 5.1

Exhibit 5.1
Ratings for Tunisia, 1994–2000

	1994	*1995*	*1996*	*1997*	*1998*	*1999*	*2000*
R&I*	BBB+	BBB+	BBB+	BBB+	BBB+	BBB+	BBB+
IBCA		BBB-	BBB-	BBB-	BBB-	BBB-	BBB-
Moody's		Baa3	Baa3	Baa3	Baa3	Baa3	Baa3
Standard & Poor's				BBB-	BBB-	BBB-	BBB

* Japan, formerly JBRI.

Source: Banque Centrale de Tunisie.

Created in 1958, BCT began its operations in the same year the Tunisian dinar was first circulated. In 1994 new legislation reinforced and extended the central bank's regulatory and supervisory powers over the banking and financial sectors.

In terms of regulation, BCT is expressly entitled to set up the rules and principles of book keeping, management and prudential norms. Banks must disclose to BCT their audited results and material facts that may pose a threat to their operations or to their depositors' interests. The auditors must also submit an activity report to the central bank at the end of each fiscal year, as well as another report to the departments of the audited bank.

The central bank's powers are wide. As well as powers of control over banks, BCT can also exercise authority and take action on bank subsidiaries, the corporates that control them, as well as that corporate's other subsidiaries.

After due warning BCT may serve injunctions on any bank, demanding it to, for example, alter its capital structure or calling for a ban on any distribution of dividends.

To protect the interests of the banking system, third parties or a bank's depositors, the central bank governor is entitled to take several actions. These include inviting the bank's shareholders to provide the bank with necessary support, organising contributions from all banks and appointing a temporary administrator.

Monetary policy

Prudent management of monetary policy, operated by BCT, has financed economic growth and reduced inflation. It has also given credibility to the monetary authorities. The state maintains a firm grip on the central bank and the banking system. The central bank may take up – at banks and bodies specially approved by the Ministry of Finance – on its proposal, bills and claims on enterprises and individuals under terms it deems necessary for the achievement of monetary policy objectives. In regulating the monetary market, BCT may buy or take up at banks, negotiable public bills as well as any claim or security on certain enterprises and individuals.

Monetary policy operated by BCT aims to preserve the value of the dinar by keeping the inflation rate as low as that of its trading partners and competitors. The intermediary objective is to match the money supply growth with the growth of economic activity (see Exhibit 5.2).

Exhibit 5.2
Financial system balance, 1998–2001 (TD million unless otherwise indicated)

	Actual			*Forecasts*		*Change (%)*	
	Dec 1998	*Dec 1999*	*Oct 2000**	*2000*	*2001*	*Dec 2000/ Dec 1999*	*Dec 2001/ Dec 2000*
Aggregate M4	14,836	16,235	16,784	17,063	17,913	5.1	5.0
Money supply M3	11,639	13,807	14,862	15,236	16,688	10.3	9.5
Money supply M2	10,726	12,816	13,812	14,194	15,571	10.8	9.7
M3 – M2	913	991	1,050	1,042	1,117	5.1	7.2
M4 – M3	3,197	2,428	1,922	1,827	1,225	-24.8	-33.0
Other resources	6,524	6,887	7,845	7,460	8,092	8.3	8.5
Resources = counterparts	21,360	23,122	24,629	24,523	26,005	6.1	6.0
Net foreign claims**	1,373	1,841	1,805	2,052	2,382	211.0	330.0
Domestic credit in wider sense	19,987	21,281	22,824	22,471	23,623	5.6	5.1
Net claims on state**	4,112	4,170	3,778	3,846	3,394	-324	-452.0
Financing of the economy	15,875	17,111	19,046	18,625	20,229	8.8	8.6

* Provisional figures.
** Variations in TD million.

Source: Banque Centrale de Tunisie.

Interest rates play a vital role in monetary policy by mobilising savings and maximising the allocation of resources. Therefore, the monetary market rate is used as a reference point by banks fixing interest rates for loans and savings. Banks are free to fix interest rates.

Banks can exchange liquidity on the money market, regulated by BCT, which intervenes to supply or mop up liquidity. The Treasury finances itself at market conditions through issuing Treasury bonds.

Excess liquidity poses a challenge

According to the IMF, the major challenge for the monetary authorities in the short term is to mop up excess liquidity that may result from a major wave of new privatisations. In the medium term, the development and diversification of Tunisia's economy and financial markets should allow BCT to rely more on interest rates as an instrument of monetary policy (see Exhibit 5.3). Reforms and strengthening of the banking system could lay the foundations for the development of the money market.

Exhibit 5.3
Monetary policy instruments and rates in force at end-2000

Rate	*%*
Tapping	5.8125
Call for tenders (TAO)	5.8750
Injection	5.9375
Allowance uptakes for 7 days	6.8750
Day-to-day money market (TM)	5.8750
Money market average rate (TMM) for November 2000	5.8750
Saving remuneration rate (TRE) for December 2000	3.8750
Reserve requirement	2.0000

Source: Banque Centrale de Tunisie.

The financial system: structure and reforms

Establishing an efficient financial system is a key component of macroeconomic policy. Officials say the financial sector will be fully liberalised over the next few years and progress has been made in restructuring public sector banks and in reinforcing prudential regulations in the banking sector. The structure of the financial system is shown in Exhibit 5.4

Commercial banks

Tunisia has 14 commercial banks that collect deposits and dispense loans in several structures for various entities. They also provide cash and exchange services and ensure international trade transactions.

Tunisian banks are listed below:

- Arab Tunisian Bank (ATB);
- Banque Franco-Tunisienne (BFT);
- Banque Nationale Agricole (BNA);
- Banque du Sud (BS);
- Banque de Tunisie (BT);
- Amen Bank;
- Banque Internationale Arabe de Tunisie (BIAT);
- Société Tunisienne de Banque (STB);
- Union Bancaire pour le Commerce et l'Industrie (UBCI);
- Union Internationale de Banques (UIB);
- Banque de l'Habitat (BH);
- Banque Tunisienne de Solidarité (BTS);

Exhibit 5.4

Structure of the financial system

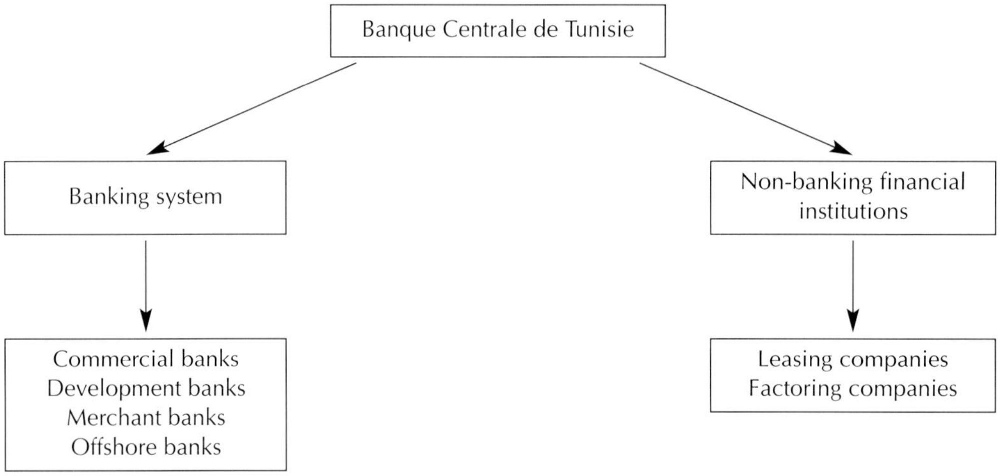

STB, one of Tunisia's commercial banks

Foreign banks in Tunisia at the end of 2000 were:

- Citibank (onshore branch);
- Arab Banking Corporation (ABC) (onshore branch).

Development banks

Six development banks extend mainly long- and medium-term loans and, under certain conditions short-term loans. They also participate in enterprise capital and collect deposits for non-residents. The banks are:

- Banque Tuniso-Koweïtienne de Développement (BTKD);
- Société Tuniso-Saoudienne d'Investissement et de Développement (STUSID);
- Banque Tuniso-Qatari d'Investissement (BTQI);
- Banque de Tunisie et des Emirats d'Investissement (BTEI);
- Banque Arabe Tuniso-Libyenne de Développement et de Commerce Extérieur (BTLD);
- Banque de Coopération du Maghreb Arabe (BCMA).

Offshore banks

Eight offshore banks collect deposits for non-residents for whom they also provide assistance in respect of foreign securities and subscriptions to borrowings. They also handle exchange and foreign trade transactions for resident customers. Under certain conditions, they collect funds and give loans in dinars. The banks are:

- Beit Ettamouil Saoudi Tounsi (BEST Bank);
- North Africa International Bank (NAIB);
- Alubaf International Bank (ALUBAF);
- Union Tunisienne de Banques (UTB);
- Tunis International Bank (TIB);
- Loan and Investment Co (LINC);
- Citibank (offshore branch);
- Arab Banking Corporation (ABC).

Merchant banks

Two merchant banks provide a range of services generally aimed at financing the creation, development and restructuring of enterprises:

- International Maghreb Merchant Bank (IMB);
- Banque d'Affaires de Tunisie (BAT).

Leasing companies

Nine leasing companies provide finance for equipment for business purposes to commercial operators that have the option to purchase leased equipment at the end of the contract:

- Tunisie Leasing;
- Union Tunisienne de Leasing;
- Compagnie Internationale de Leasing;
- Arab Tunisian Leasing;
- Amen Lease;
- General Leasing;
- Modern Leasing;
- Arab International Lease;
- BEST Lease.

Factoring companies

Two factoring companies purchase from clients trade receivables, which they collect:

- Tunisie Factoring;
- Unifactor.

Inefficiencies in the system

Several inefficiencies in the financial system are deep rooted. The burden of non-performing loans remains high, at 20 per cent of GDP in 1999, and this continues to affect the cost of financing. If the allocation of credit is to be improved and the risk of accumulating new bad loans contained, greater corporate transparency will be required, especially in terms of accounting, financial reporting, and enterprises' ownership structures.

Capital markets continue to play a very marginal role in financing the economy in comparison with bank credit. Some measures to promote capital markets have been introduced but more are needed to mobilise foreign and domestic savings. Determined efforts to reform the insurance market are in train and should promote institutional saving.

Reforms

Efforts to reform the financial system and banking sector are driven by the need to improve the range and quality of products and services on offer from domestic banks. They will be up against tough competition from foreign banks as the sector opens up under the Association Agreement with the European Union.

Several reforms have aimed to create a more flexible, transparent and entrepreneurial banking sector. Notable reforms and events in the financial system during 2000 included three amendments enacted in April to legislation determining BCT's operations.

The first amendment allows the central bank to uptake a new product – bonds equivalent to Treasury bonds (BTAs) – introduced in March 1999 by the state in a bid to modernise instruments of internal debt. These new bonds are medium- and long-term borrowing securities and therefore fell out of bounds for BCT prior to April 2000 when the law restricted it to securities with less than six months' maturity. Under this amendment BCT can buy or make allowance uptake of these new securities from banks whatever their maturity.

This allows BCT more flexibility in conducting monetary policy by expanding its repertoire of interventions, hence enabling it to act more efficiently on bank liquidity and control over interest rates on the money market.

A taste for Japanese paper

The central bank has also been active on international markets. After a three-year absence, it returned to the Japanese market in July 2000 when it issued an innovative global Samurai bond deal, one of the first to accommodate both Japanese and non-Japanese investors.

Moody's Investors Service assigned Baa3 ratings to a ¥35,000 million bond due in 2010 and a ¥15,000 million bond due in 2030. The 30-year tranche was aimed at investors looking to diversify their portfolio risks by investing in the Tunisian bonds. These investors have usually only shown interest in bonds from issuers rated AA or higher.

From 1994 to 1997, BCT issued six samurai bonds with maturities of between five and 20 years, thereby establishing with Japanese investors a reputation that was enhanced when two of these issues were reimbursed in February and April 2000 for a total of ¥40 billion. In December 2000, BCT returned again to the capital markets when it issued a private investment of ¥10 billion with a maturity of 18 months.

Controlling consumer loans

In the second amendment BCT has been given new powers to keep a central registry of consumer loans made by banks, finance companies, and retailers. Lenders who comply with BCT's reporting requirements will be able to run credit checks on clients. This amendment aims to prevent consumers running up excessive debts and responds to steep increases in loans to private individuals over recent years.

Electronic clearing

The third amendment paved the way for BCT to participate in the equity of Société Interbancaire de Télécompensation (SIBTEL – electronic-clearing interbank company). The introduction of an electronic clearing system has been seen as a critical element in modernising the banking sector and aims to reduce the time taken to clear payments to less than 48 hours, wherever payment is presented. Prior to the introduction of the new clearing system in December 1999, payments had taken around 14 days to clear, thereby deterring use of the banking system.

As a user of, and the authority responsible for, the new payment system, it was deemed desirable for BCT to participate in its capital. The third amendment removed the bar that had previously forbidden the central bank taking equity positions. As well as participating in the capital of SIBTEL, the central bank can also take an equity position in any other company providing an interbanking service in the future.

Commercial banks: consolidation and mergers

Tunisia's commercial banks are shaping up to tougher competition in a liberalised financial sector by installing new technologies and developing more effective management and operating structures. To raise the cash required to make these investments, banks are opening up to foreign investors that may also bring valuable technological resources and capabilities. They are also looking for consolidation and merger opportunities to make operations more efficient and to increase their attractiveness to the markets.

Some banks have reported soaring growth. Net profit at Banque de Tunisie (BT) rose 38 per cent to TD10.18 million in the first half of 2000 compared with the same six months in 1999. The bank's assets in the first half of 2000 stood at TD1.16 billion compared with TD1.01 billion in the same period in 1999.

Tunisia's largest bank, Banque Nationale Agricole (BNA), reported less spectacular half-year results. It reported net profit up 6.7 per cent to TD10.05 million in the first half of 2000 compared with the same period in 1999. Assets were at TD2.64 billion for the January-June period compared with TD2.48 billion in the first six months of 1999.

Several state-owned banks have been fully or partially privatised. Banque du Sud (BS) was partially privatised in 1997. It has accumulated total assets of TD1,256 million (1999), a network of 86 branches and several financial and investment services subsidiaries. It has looked overseas to developing its activities by forging a partnership with Italy's Monte Dei Paschi Di Siena. The Italian bank has been considering increasing its stake in the Tunisian bank.

Exhibit 5.5

BIAT ownership at 31 December 2000

Institution	*Stake (%)*
Bank of New York	13.57
Istituto Bancaire San Paolo Di Torino	5.61
Wafabank (Morocco)	2.86
Abu Dhabi Investment Authority	2.14
The National Commercial Bank Of Jeddah	1.56
Al Ahly Bank Of Kuwait	1.71
Société Marseillaise De Crédit (France)	1.60
Caisse Centrale Des Banques Populaires (France)	1.60
Bank Of Kuwait And The Middle East	0.67
Others	3.45

Source: BIAT.

BIAT internationalises

Another bank in which foreign institutions have gained significant positions by acquiring 34.77 per cent of its capital is Banque Internationale Arabe de Tunisie (BIAT) (see Exhibit 5.5). Until very recently Tunisia's largest private bank, BIAT posted half-yearly profits of TD13.13 million to June 2000, up 22.52 per cent compared with the same period in 1999. Assets at BIAT stood at TD2.09 billion for the period compared with TD1.63 billion for the first half of 1999. In 1999 net profit was TD25.3 million, an increase of 19.84 per cent over 1998.

BIAT is seen as one of Tunisia's more innovative and soundly managed banks. It holds key positions in the credit and debit cards as well as the ATM market. A modernisation programme over recent years has seen BIAT build a new head office, overhaul its branch network, upgrade its information systems and take on a new brand identity for marketing purposes.

Banks have been investing in technology to keep competitive. BIAT recently announced it would replace its mainframe with open systems supplied by PeerLogic and Sun Microsystems to provide faster and better customer service. The scaleable system will service the bank's 100-branch network throughout Tunisia and add five branches each year. The new system should allow BIAT to take advantage of future e-business opportunities for international growth.

Amen Bank and BNA explore the new economy

Recognised as one of the country's more progressive institutions, Amen Bank was the first in Tunisia to launch an internet banking service. Since June 1999 clients have been able to consult their accounts and make transfers, order cheque-books, authorise payments to third parties and access information on the bourse and financial markets. Amen Bank also provides a comprehensive range of fax and telephone banking services. The bank has said its budget for upgrading its information systems and services is TD15 million.

Another venturer in the new economy is BNA which has a stake in BNA-Capitaux, a Tunisian website that provides financial reports and analyses of performance on the local securities

Amen Bank was the first bank in Tunisia to launch an internet banking service

market. The website also provides live broadcasts direct from the Tunis stock exchange. BNA claims to be Tunisia's largest brokerage with a 15 per cent market share in trading and 26,000 private and institutional investors, both local and foreign. It became the first brokerage company to be electronically connected to the domestic stock exchange.

Merger trend

A long-awaited merger of three state-owned Tunisian banks was completed in December 2000. Banque Nationale de Développement Touristique (BNDT) and Banque de Développement Economique de Tunisie (BDET) are both now subsumed in commercial bank Société Tunisienne de Banque (STB) under whose name the merged bank now operates.

The STB board decided a TD44.3 million increase in capital through the issue of 8.86 million shares in return for contributions of one BDET share for 0.64 STB share and one BNDT share for 0.41 STB share. The merged bank becomes the country's largest in terms of assets and, structured around STB, the biggest of the three banks with end-1999 assets of TD2.36 billion. This compares with TD755 million for BDET and TD538 million for BNDT. The state retains a majority stake of about 50 per cent in the new bank with the remainder shared by domestic and foreign investors.

Another merger has failed at the last hurdle. Commercial bank, Union Internationale de Banque (UIB) and Banque de Tunisie et des Emirats pour l'Investissement (BTEI), the joint state bank with the United Arab Emirates had been due to merge by the beginning of 2001. The merger was called off in December 2000 but is expected to continue. According to BCT former governor, Mohammed Béji Hamda:

> Thirteen commercial banks is now perhaps a little too much, and so some consolidation could follow, but it is important to remember that, already, the big three banks hold 45 per cent of total assets in the domestic banking sector – there is thus already a concentration in the system.

Foreign banks: Citibank digs in, ABC expands

Two foreign banks have set up commercial operations in Tunisia, Citibank of the United States and Bahrain-based Arab Banking Corporation (ABC).

For nearly a decade Citibank was the only 100 per cent foreign-owned onshore bank in Tunisia. It established an offshore branch in 1987 and in 1989 it was licensed to operate as a resident bank. In 1991 a Citibank branch opened in Sfax.

Citigroup has operated in Tunisia through Citibank NA Tunisia since 1978. It became a full-service corporate and investment bank in 1989 and since 1997 it has earned a solid reputation in the market as a consumer bank.

With two branches – one in Tunis and the other in Sfax, it was the first bank to provide both onshore and offshore activities. In the early 1990s, the bank focused on treasury services and continues to play a critical role in development of Tunisia's financial sector. It has cultivated a customer base of large multinationals and domestic corporates, and doubled its revenues in 1999.

Citibank was the first foreign exchange dealer in Tunisian dinar, and consequently contributes to the liquidity of the market. It is also a leading provider of cash management products and was called in to help BCT automate its clearing system.

The US bank is clear about its Tunisian strategy. It has adapted its services to the Tunisian market where it operates in several segments, including the interbank network, payment cards and credit cards. Citibank plans to grow its branch network, expand its corporate customer base to include small- and medium-sized enterprises and leverage more investment banking opportunities. It also has regional aspirations, with positions in Algeria and Morocco.

Citibank maintains it is Tunisia's primary and most active foreign bank, and it is set to lead the country's banking sector. The US group will compete for these positions with the largest banking group in the Arab world.

An onshore ABC subsidiary opened in Tunis in June 2000. With capital of TD18 million, ABC Tunisie provides a full range of retail and commercial banking services to corporate and private clients. An ABC Tunisie branch network is to be rolled out throughout the country's major cities.

Prior to obtaining an onshore banking licence, ABC had an offshore banking unit in Tunisia, which is expected to remain operational until 2003. The offshore operation has been successful in building a good image for ABC's new operation, and a ready-made prime customer base and network of contacts in the local banking system.

Development banks and other investment instruments

Tunisia hosts six development banks operated as joint ventures between the government and friendly Arab states. These fulfilled an important role in the past, when they helped to recycle oil boom and other funds into industrial, tourism and other development projects within Tunisia. According to BCT former governor, Mohammed Béji Hamda:

> The development banks were very useful in the period after independence, but we are now reviewing their role … as was implied in the [failed] UIB/BTEI merger … . In the new environment, finding a solution to the future of the development banks is our top priority.

On the domestic front, the STB, BDET and BNDT merger will go a long way towards answering these questions.

Sophisticated investment vehicles now join conventional bilateral and multinational institutions in providing both public and private sector development finance. In 1999 Tunisia benefited from bilateral external financing totalling TD284 million, of which Japan provided TD117 million, France advanced TD109 million while the remaining TD58 million came from several other sources.

Multilateral support

Multilateral institutions, comprising the World Bank, the Arab Fund for Economic and Social Development (AFESD), the European Investment Bank (EIB) and the African Development Bank (AfDB) and others provided TD527 million in external finance in 1999. Consolidation and privatisations in the reform process have been backed by loans and grants worth about US$300 million from the World Bank, the European Union (EU) and the AfDB.

This scale of activity reflects the fact that, although no longer among the less-developed countries, Tunisia can still draw on substantial multilateral funds for development projects – helped by its good reputation for delivering completion dates on time and its relatively high absorption capacity.

In 2000, the World Bank committed US$99 million to the Education Quality Improvement Programme (EQIP) to support the government's efforts to provide near universal basic education, offer more students access to higher education and improve the quality of education in several other areas. It also approved a US$103 million loan for the Water Sector Investment Project to promote effective integrated water resource management and to promote water resources conservation and environmental protection.

Three agricultural development programmes will benefit from loans approved in November 2000 by the AfDB. The programmes in Gabès, Gafsa and Kasserine will receive loans of €16.1 million, €16.7 million and €15.4 million respectively. The AfDB loans totalling €48.2 million will finance 95.1 per cent of the foreign exchange costs and part of the local currency expenses of the project whose total cost amounts to €81.8 million. AfDB operations in Tunisia started in 1968 and in 71 operations, the group has committed a total of US$2.72 billion, of which about US$2.10 billion has been disbursed.

In November 2000, the EIB advanced two loans totalling €70 million for energy and environmental infrastructure. A loan of €25 million supports the construction of nine controlled landfills and 17 waste transfer centres. Gas and electricity utility, Société Tunisienne de l'Électricité et du Gaz (STEG) has been advanced €45 million for schemes to expand the power transmission and supply network throughout the country.

Earlier in the year the EIB advanced the first two loans to be made available to a partner Mediterranean country under the new mandate entrusted to the EIB over the period 2000-2006. Société Nationale des Chemins de Fer Tunisiens (SNCFT) has been advanced €25 million towards track doubling of the line between Tunis and Sousse and modernisation of the rail network in the Sousse area. The private sector benefits from a €25 million advance for medium- and long-term financing of companies in the production and services sectors undergoing restructuring in the *mise à niveau* (upgrading) programme and investing in expansion and modernisation of their activities.

Investment funds

Tunisia can also tap into a new investment fund creatively constructed by private and public investors. The Maghreb Private Equity Fund opened in June 2000 with commitments of US$21 million and hopes to raise this to US$35 million. The initial tranche of public and private investors comprised:

- US$5 million from the World Bank's International Finance Corporation;
- €5 million from EIB;
- US$3 million from Proparco, the French private sector development agency;
- US$3 million Seco from a Swiss development agency;
- US$3 million from FMO, the Dutch development agency; and
- US$2 million from Natexis Banques Populaires, the newly formed investment subsidiary of France's Banques Populaires group.

Other potential fund shareholders are European and North African corporate investors. Funds will be invested in Morocco (at least 70 per cent of the fund), in Tunisia and in Algeria (maximum 30 per cent of the fund), the average amount totalling Ffr2-3 million.

The fund is managed by Maghreb Invest Management Limited, owned by Tunisia's Tuninvest Finance Group, stockbrokers Upline Securities of Morocco, French investment fund Natexis Banques Populaires Group, as well as by SFI and FMO. With funds amounting to US$50 million, Tuninvest is the main investment capital fund manager in Tunisia.

The capital market

The stock exchange

An unassuming office block in a modest part of the capital is the location of the Bourse des Valeurs Mobilières de Tunis (BVMT – the Tunis stock exchange). By international standards it is small and quiet. As a vehicle for financing the commercial motors of Tunisia's economy and stimulating domestic and foreign, private and institutional participation in the capital markets, it is seen as an integral dimension of the economic framework.

It also aspires to become part of Tunisia's social fabric, with a participative culture, reflected in a room adjacent to the trading floor where the public watches the ticker go by on a large screen. Differing from bullish Anglo-Saxon or Latin exchanges, but in keeping with Tunisia's inclusive policies such as equality for women, universal access to education and the establishment of a majority middle class, the bourse is a facility in which all Tunisians are encouraged to participate. A declared objective of the BVMT is to provide all Tunisians with access to the stock market, hence Tunisians become employers and employees at the same time.

The success of the bourse is also important for continuing Tunisia's economic growth, and it must start to provide finance for the country's stock of enterprises that are currently far too reliant on bank finance. In this context, reform-led cultural change is called for.

Fiscal advantages introduced in February 1999 have aimed to encourage new companies to participate in the capital market and already-listed companies to open up additional share capital to the public. New participants may obtain 20–35 per cent discounts on their corporate income tax bill for five years if they list a minimum of 30 per cent of their capital on the bourse.

More reforms will be needed to attract companies to the stock exchange. Listed companies must file quarterly accounts, a requirement that falls outside many Tunisian business' culture. Moreover, credit is relatively cheap and for companies without sufficient capitalisation and external ratings to gain automatic stock market accreditation, the process of obtaining the required prime bank guarantee is expensive. Barriers to stock market entry need to be lowered and the motivation to list needs to be heightened.

Several recent reforms have aimed to raise the structures and systems of Tunisia's capital markets to international standards. These include:

- the privatisation of the stock exchange;
- the establishment of the Conseil de Marché Financier (CMF – the Capital Market Council), an autonomous regulatory and supervisory body that regulates the markets and supervises transactions in order to protect investors;
- the establishment of clearing house STICODEVAM, which also serves as a central depository to hold securities; and
- a capital market guarantee fund, managed by the stock exchange, which now covers stockbrokers against counterparty risks.

Officials say the financial sector will be fully liberalised over the next few years

The establishment of an electronic quotation system has transformed the speed and efficiency of the market's operations. The exchange uses a trading platform derived from the French SUPERCAC electronic trading system, which delivers price transparency and real-time price quotations on Reuters. Reorganisation and the introduction of new technologies have resulted in a more transparent and secure market.

Tunisia's sober approach to business and economic management is evident in stock exchange rules. These state that the main index has an acceptable variation of 4.5 per cent. Beyond that, the exchange closes for that day. The equitable spirit of the rule allows investors time to respond to fluctuations, with the added benefit of guarding the market from speculators.

New financial products

Efforts to breathe life into the stock exchange have been successful. New financial products launched by the state – short-term Treasury bonds (BTCTs), bonds equivalent to Treasury bonds (BTAs) and the stock-savings account (Compte Epargne Action – CEA) have stimulated supplies of stocks and bonds. Tunisians can regularly pay small sums into a CEA for five years, over which time half the amount that they contribute up to a specified limited may be tax deductible.

Participation in the market has increased. Offerings through public calls for savings recorded TD1.68 billion in 1999, nine times higher than the amount raised in the previous year and the highest since 1990 (see Exhibit 5.6). This upturn was due solely to the BTCT and BTA offerings. The volume of share and bond offerings by companies remained low. In the same year the volume of savings mobilised through the primary market firmed up, accounting for 26.9 per cent of total national savings and 26.2 per cent of gross investment compared with 3.5 per cent and 3.4 per cent respectively in 1998.

Exhibit 5.6

Main historical stock market indicators

Description	*1995*	*1996*	*1997*	*1998*	*1999*
Volume of offerings through public call for savings (TD million)	480.0	357.0	493.0	190.0	1,708.5**
Volume of offerings through public call for savings/national savings (%)	14.0	8.3	10.1	3.6	27.5
Volume of public offerings through public call for savings/gross investment (%)	11.6	8.1	9.6	3.6	26.5
Stock market capitalisation/GDP (%)	23.3	20.4	12.6	10.8	13.5
Overall volume of transactions	927.0	626.0	590.0	915.0	880.0
of which : stock market quotation	684.0	274.0	287.0	237.0	554.0
Liquidity rate (%)	61.0	12.0	36.0	37.0	46.0
Assets managed by investment companies	1,138.0	1,051.0	1,237.0	1,477.0	1,774.0
of which : SICAV* (TD million)	622.0	521.0	681.0	872.0	1,102.0

*Sociétés d'Investissement à Capital Variable — Variable Capital Investment Trusts (Unit trusts).

** of which TD759.5 million are BTCTs.

Sources: Tunis Stock Exchange (BVMT) and the Capital Market Council (CMF).

A bull market among the bears

After two years in the doldrums, in 1998 some investment trusts began to show gains. These gains continued through the following year and into 2000 – when Tunis was the best performing African market in a lack lustre year for trading worldwide. These well performing trusts included the most popular of investment vehicles, Sociétés d'Investissement à Capital Variable (SICAV – Variable Capital Investment Trusts), which were introduced in 1995. The performance of Sociétés d'Investissement à Capital Risque (SICAR – Risk Capital Investment Trusts) also picked up in 1998 as a result of stock market recovery.

Some investment funds may be mixed and a third investment vehicle is also available in the form of Sociétés d'Investissement à Capital Fixe (SICAF – Fixed Capital Investment Trusts).

Market history and structure

Established in 1969 the Tunis Stock Exchange was privatised in 1995 with the capital divided equally between 28 brokers firms through which all deals are transacted. Listed companies include private and state-owned companies as well as jointly private and state-owned enterprises.

There were 44 listed companies at end-2000:

Banks:
- Amen Bank (AB);
- Arab Tunisian Bank (ATB);
- Banque de Développement Economique de Tunisie (BDET);
- Banque de l'Habitat (BH);
- Banque de Tunisie (BT);
- Banque de Tunisie et des Emirats d'Investissement (BTEI);
- Banque du Sud (BS);
- Banque Internationale Arabe de Tunisie (BIAT);
- Banque Nationale Agricole (BNA);
- Banque Nationale de Développement Touristique (BNDT);
- Société Tunisienne de Banque (STB);
- Union Bancaire pour le Commerce & l'Industrie (UBCI);
- Union Internationale de Banques (UIB).

Insurance:
- Compagnie d'Assurances et de Réassurances (ASTREE);
- Société Tunisienne d'Assurances et de Réassurances (STAR);
- Compagnie d'Assurances et de Réassurances Tuniso-Européenne (CARTE).

Leasing:
- Amen Lease (ALS);
- Arab Tunisian Lease (ATL);
- Compagnie Internationale de Leasing (CIL);

- General Leasing (GL);
- Tunisie Leasing (TLS).

Investment:
- Placements de Tunisie (PLTU – SICAF portfolio);
- Société de Placement & de Développement Industriel et Touristique (SPDIT – SICAF);
- Tuninvest (TINV – SICAR).

Retail and distribution:
- Société HELA d'Electro-ménagers & de Confort (BATAM);
- Société Magasin Général (SMG);
- Société Tunisienne des Marchés de Gros (SOTUMAG);
- Société Nouvelle Maison de la Ville de Tunis – Monoprix (MNP).

Industrials:
- Air Liquide Tunisie (AL);
- Société Chimique (ALKIMIA);
- Les Ateliers Mécaniques du Sahel (AMS);
- Société des Industries Chimiques du Fluor (ICF);
- Le Moteur (MTR);
- Société Frigorifique et Brasserie de Tunis (SFBT);
- Société Industrielle d'Appareillage et de Matériels Electriques(SIAME);
- Société Tunisienne de Verreries (SOTUVER);
- Société de Produits Chimiques Détergents (SPCD);
- Société Tunisienne de l'Industrie Laitière (STIL);
- Tunisie Lait (TLAIT).

Tourism:
- Palm Beach Hotels Tunisia (PBHT).

Construction:
- Société Immobilière et de Participations (SIMPAR).

Transport:
- Société Tunisienne de l'Air (TUNISAIR).

Telecoms:
- Société Tunisienne d'Entreprises de Télécommunications (SOTETEL).

Agribusiness:
- Société El Mazraa.

Exhibit 5.7

BVMT Index 2001: Stocks – (ranked in order of trading frequency)

1. ATL
2. BIAT
3. TUNISIE LEASING
4. BH
5. STB
6. BS
7. SFBT
8. TUNISAIR
9. BATAM
10. GENERAL LEASING
11. SOTUMAG
12. SIAME
13. SOTETEL
14. BT
15. CIL
16. UIB
17. UBCI
18. BNA
19. MONOPRIX
20. AL MAZRAA
21. MAGASIN GENERAL
22. AMEN BANK
23. ATB
24. AMS
25. AMEN LEASE

Source: BVMT.

Indices

Stock exchange performance is measured by two indices. The BVMT Index contains all the ordinary shares – excluding portfolio investment companies with high trading frequencies. The list is revisited each year and in 2001 contained 25 stocks (see Exhibit 5.7)

The broader Tunindex is an index containing all stocks listed for more than six months, excluding non-ordinary shares and portfolio investment companies.

Performance and market dynamics

Tunisia's stock exchange is now considered one of the best performing in Africa and the Arab world. It recorded stellar gains in 1999 and 2000 after lacklustre performances in 1997 and 1998.

The BVMT Index picked up considerably in 1999, closing the year with a gain of 74 per cent and in 2000 it soared by nearly 76 per cent (see Exhibit 5.8). However, more modest gains by the broader Tunindex of nearly 21 per cent in 2000 and 30 per cent in 1999 reveal some structural weaknesses in the stock exchange.

The central bank has attributed the disproportionate progress of the Tunindex and BVMT indices in 1999 to a sharp rise in stock prices for companies with weak capitalisation. Conversely, well-capitalised ventures, notably bank stocks, which account for only 60 per cent of the sample chosen for the Tunindex, increased only moderately.

The stock market remains small and unrepresentative of Tunisia's economy. With a total market capitalisation of just TD3.9 billion at 31 December 2000, it lists very few companies in the sectors that fuel Tunisia's economic growth, and a preponderance of financial and banking stocks in a sector that is not the best-honed component in the country's economic structure.

Out of the 25 stocks in the BVMT Index, only half a dozen produce value-added goods or services. The financial sectors' share of total market capitalisation in 1999 was 65.1 per cent, compared with the industrial sector with just an 18.8 per cent share.

While foreign capital has driven Tunisia's traditional industries such as textiles, manufacturing industries and tourism, it has only recently started to flow at any significant rate

Exhibit 5.8

Stock market performance, 1995–2000

	1995	*1996*	*1997*	*1998*	*1999*	*2000*
BVMT index in points (base 100 on 30 September 1990, adjusted on 31 March 1998 to 465.77)	634.71	570.64	455.64	464.56	810.24	1,424.91
Tunindex in points (base 1,000 on 31 December 1997)	–	–	1.000	917.08	1,192.57	1,442.61
Stock market capitalisation (TD million)	3,967	3,892	2,632	2,450	3,360	3,889

Source: BVMT.

into the stock market. Foreign investors are entitled to participate in up to 50 per cent of company capital, more if authorised.

Foreign investments in the stock exchange at end-2000 represented no more than around 21 per cent of total market capital. Over a dozen listed companies have less than 1 per cent of foreign capital, some have none and only a handful of listed companies have a significant proportion of foreign investment (see Exhibit 5.9).

Foreign investors may be beguiled by the modernity of Tunisia's bourse and impressed by its recent performance. Size matters, however, if it is to attract serious institutional interest and revitalise small investor interest.

Exhibit 5.9

Listed companies with high levels of foreign ownership at 31 December 2000

Company	*Foreign ownership (% of total ownership)*
SPCT*	99.00
ATB	64.24
Air Liquide Tunisie	59.36
UBCI	50.38
SFBT	48.28
ASTREE	48.82
BNDT	42.96

* Unilever subsidiary.

Source: BVMT.

No new companies were quoted on the stock exchange in 2000 but in 1999, six new companies appeared, four from the public sector. Small investors showed particular enthusiasm for these stocks, which were up to seven times oversubscribed, and the secondary market took off. The companies are:

- Société Tunisienne de Verreries (SOTUVER), a manufacturer of glass and glass substitute products;
- Société Héla d'Électroménager et de Confort, a distributor of electrical, household and luxury goods;
- Société Magasin Général, a bulk supplier of agricultural produce, groceries and equipment;
- General Leasing, a leasing company;
- Société Industrielle d'Appareillages et de Matériels Électriques (SIAME), a manufacturer and distributor of electronic and electrical equipment; and
- Société Tunisienne des Marchés de GROS (SOTUMAG), a market management company.

One of the more exciting events in 2000 came in November with the acquisition of two Tunisian companies by Unilever subsidiary, Norda B.V. The Anglo-Dutch food giant received government approval to acquire majority stakes in Tunisia's Codepar and Société de Produits Chimiques et Detergents (SPCD). Both companies are traded on the bourse. Norda invested about TD88 million in the acquisition of Codepar and TD15.8 million for 313,734 shares for an initial 25 per cent in SPCD. At the time of the acquisition Codepar controlled 58 per cent of SPCD.

More listings across more sectors are needed. These may emerge on the market as a result of the ambitious 2001 privatisation programme. If this happens, the stock exchange may find itself included in the IFC and Morgan Stanley emerging market indices, used extensively by institutional investors in the US and Europe.

For all its flaws, there are rewards on the Tunisian bourse for investors. Privatised telecommunications engineering firm, SOTETEL, has seen its shares trade at values 10 times higher than the 1999 offer price.

6 *Investment: fuelling the economy*

Growth drivers

The attraction of investment has played a central role in Tunisian economic policy for more than a decade. More than most other Arab/African economies, Tunisia has understood that the benefits of the sort of structural adjustment advocated by the IMF and other donors since the 1980s should be reflected in a significant upturn in private investment. This would benefit from the much improved business environment and provide the foundation stones on which a stable economy is built.

Foreign direct investment (FDI) in the production sector is rightly given credit for driving economic growth. However, its positive contribution has and continues to be supported by prudent public spending on capital works, often boosted by significant sums from multilateral and bilateral donors. The government has deployed considerable resources to focus strongly on attracting FDI, with an active ministry dedicated to attracting investment – not least by coordinating detailed studies to give Tunisia a competitive edge – and the creation of a dynamic Foreign Investment Promotion Agency (FIPA). Through its Tunis operation and a number of offices abroad, including in London and Washington, FIPA can play a significant role in attracting investors. Certainly, compared with the representatives of so many other countries now vying for FDI, the understanding of global business displayed by Tunisian officials working in the investment business should provide a very positive signal to potential investors.

An increasing volume of investment now derives from private domestic investors and the reinvestment of profits by Tunisia's stock of enterprises, the sum of which is now substantial. Investment by smaller companies is often levered by government support. The availability of grants under the *mise à niveau* (upgrading) programme and other initiatives has prompted several hundreds of smaller investments to improve the assets and thereby the quality and level of productivity in domestic firms.

Foreign direct investment

Tunisia's stability and favourable business environment have resulted in strong FDI flows. Representing 10 per cent of productive investments, they have primed activities responsible for generating one-third of exports and one-sixth of total employment. More than 2,000 foreign

View of Mohammed V Avenue, Tunis

firms from over 50 countries have started operations in Tunisia. Between them they have generated 192,000 jobs.

A total of 181 wholly or partially foreign-owned firms started operations in Tunisia in 2000. Between them they created 14,751 jobs. FDI in 2000 amounted to TD1.03 billion, up from TD437.2 million in 1999. FDI for 2001 was estimated at TD900 million. To give an idea of the direction of Tunisian investment this would include the following components:

- the auction of a strategic stake in the country's second global system for mobiles (GSM) telephone system;
- the privatisation of Union Internationale de Banque;
- the opening of the Rades private power plant by a group led by PSEG Global of the United States, expected in September 2001;
- another 40 privatisations during 2001; and
- new projects by foreign investors – Merdassi said there were around 100 in the pipeline.

These projects should easily surpass the TD1 billion FDI threshold – even without the US$500 million gas development spending planned by British Gas Inter-national over the next three to four years, Merdassi observed.

Investments in 28 projects that had not been completed at the beginning of 2001 had reached TD165 million, and should result in the creation of 4,500 additional jobs. Investments in newly declared projects by January 2001 amounted to TD755 million for 33 projects with the potential to create more than 9,900 jobs.

Evolution of FDI

Even before steep increases in 2000 (total FDI reached TD1.03 billion), volumes of FDI had soared (see Exhibits 6.1 to 6.3 for FDI statistics). In 1999, investments amounted to TD437.2 million, a more than fivefold increase over TD77.5 million in 1990. Non-energy investments increased tenfold comparing the same years, from TD24.5 million to nearly TD242.4 million.

The steep increase in 2000 was mainly due to the sale of two cement plants to Italian and Spanish groups for a total of TD361.5 million, and the acquisition of two Tunisian firms by the Anglo-Dutch group Unilever for TD104 million.

However, most investments are much lower, as other investments announced in 2000 suggest. The sort of mega industrial or technology investment that Tunisia has worked so hard to secure remains elusive.

In 2000, Chambourcy became the latest in a line of internationally recognised food brands to start operations in Tunisia. Its agreement with domestic milk products company, Tunisie Lait, means it now joins other foreign food companies including Danone, Yoplait, and Mamie Nova.

The electrical and electronics sectors attracted two significant foreign investments in 2000, of TD5.7 million from Turkey's Arcelik and TD5 million from the parent group of Sylvania, which has now commenced manufacturing lighting products for the domestic and automotive markets.

In the plastics industry, Autoliv France has invested nearly TD2 million in a steering wheel manufacturing facility, and planned a further investment of TD5 million. A Saudi investment of TD13 million in an olive oil processing and conditioning facility by Satuco was the highlight in the agribusiness sector in 2000.

Exhibit 6.1

Evolution of FDI stock (foreign or joint stock companies)

	1990	*1999*
FDI stock (TD million)	6,339	15,262
Number of operations	906	1,960

Source: FIPA.

Exhibit 6.2

Number of foreign companies per sector, January 2000

Manufacturing	1,624
Hotels and leisure	146
Services*	90
Energy	53
Agriculture	46

* Mainly computer industry, telecommunications & consulting.

Source: FIPA.

Exhibit 6.3

FDI flow per sector, 1999

	TD million	*%*
Manufacturing	197.9	45.3
Energy	194.8	44.6
Tourism	37.2	8.5
Agriculture	3.2	0.7
Services	4.1	0.9

Source: Banque Centrale de Tunisie.

International companies, often in partnership with domestic companies, now operate in many industries and particularly in the food, computer services, automobile components, pharmaceutical, textile, shoe and leather, electrical, electromechanical, agricultural and tourism sector.

Household names with Tunisian operations include Agip, Isuzu, Lee Cooper, BG International (British Gas), Mobil, Canal Plus, Citibank, Nestlé, Coca Cola, Pirelli, Renault, Sara Lee, Esso, General Electric, Thomson Multimedia, General Motors, Total, Lucent Technologies, Unilever, Volvo, Benetton, Electrolux, Scania, Microsoft and NHK Spring.

Europe: the special relationship

Tunisia's close ties with Europe, sealed in Tunisia's Association Agreement with the European Union, have resulted in strong investments from companies based in EU member states. Proximity to the European market and a position at the forefront of the drive to create a free Euro-Mediterranean trading area provides Tunisia with distinct competitive advantages over its southern and eastern Mediterranean neighbours. Lower production costs, particularly in terms of labour, provides Tunisia with a competitive advantage over EU member states. The combination of these factors has resulted in Tunisia proving a good location for manufacturers requiring lower cost production facilities with easy access to European markets. Hence Tunisia hosts dozens of European manufacturers making components for the French, German, Italian and Swedish motor industries.

Nearly 88 per cent of foreign companies with Tunisian operations are EU-based. French firms lead with 38.1 per cent of total investments, followed by Italian firms (21.6 per cent) and German firms (12.2 per cent). Recent diversification of investment opportunities has according to FIPA stimulated investment from other countries, such as Switzerland, Belgium, the United Kingdom and Arab countries. Main origins of FDI are shown in Exhibit 6.4.

Exhibit 6.4
Main origins of FDI flows, 1999*

	(%)
France	29.8
Italy	15.2
Germany	12.1
Arab Countries	14.3
Belgium	5.5
Holland	4.0
Switzerland	3.7
Turkey	2.2
United States	7.1
Other countries	6.3

* Excluding energy.

Source: FIPA.

Rationales for investment

Structures in Tunisia's favourable investment framework include a clear investment code that applies to most sectors, adequate legal protection for investors and relatively straightforward administrative procedures managed by one agency. There are several investment incentive schemes, the most attractive of which are for 100 per cent exporting companies. Investors can freely transfer funds through the foreign exchange market.

Tunisia's continually improving infrastructure is increasingly able to support trade flows and business activities and the government has made efforts to keep factor costs in communications and energy competitive. Reduced internet tariffs became effective on 1 January 2001 for example.

Behind these formal structures Tunisia's education and vocational training provision have resulted in a highly trained workforce. A significant proportion of Tunisian students study abroad while many workers now have considerable experience working for multinational companies and corporates with operations in Tunisia. Reasonable labour costs have been a significant attraction to European and North American investors.

Another growing reason to invest in Tunisia is the quality of domestic supply chains in its major industrial sectors. Improvements in management, quality control and productivity in domestic companies makes the country an attractive proposition for investors requiring suppliers of goods and services in Tunisia's traditional industries.

A favourable legal and regulatory environment

Tunisia's reforms have focused on creating an investment framework favourable enough to attract foreign investment. It is generally transparent, liberal and efficient. Reducing tariff barriers, flexibility in the tax system, consistent rules for investment, transparency in procurement contracts and privatisations and a standardised accounting system have helped perceptions of Tunisia as a safe investment location.

According to a study by Transparency International, Tunisia ranks above all Arab countries, most African countries, and some Mediterranean countries, in terms of the transparency of its business environment (see Exhibit 6.5).

Tunisia's accounting system complies with standards according to the International Accounting Standard Committee. The tax system has undergone several overhauls. Revenues derive from direct and indirect taxes, registration duties and customs duties. A programme to dismantle tariffs is under way.

The Investment Incentives Code (IIC) is the law that governs both national and foreign investment. It confirms the freedom to invest in most sectors except mining, energy, local trade and finance. These are governed by specific legislation.

A simple declaration is required for investments in several sectors, including manufacturing, agriculture, food and public works and from businesses that exported 100 per cent of their services.

Environmental audits are required for every project related to establishing any industrial, agricultural or commercial company. Projects related to polluting activities are necessarily subject to an environmental impact study. Agriculture and food industry projects, extractive and energy industries are subject to a descriptive summary of the business and of its foreseeable environmental impact.

Authorisation must be obtained prior to investments in waste and refuse recycling and processing, fishing, tourism, transport and

Exhibit 6.5

Transparency International Rank Country Score*

Rank	Country	Score*
21	France	6.7
25	Belgium	6.1
32=	**Tunisia**	**5.2**
32=	Hungary	5.2
34	South Africa	5.0
35	Greece	4.9
39	Italy	4.6
43	Poland	4.1
50	Turkey	3.8

* Each country is scored between 0 to 10, where 10 is a high degree of transparency and 0 is a high level of corruption.

Source: Transparency International, September 2000.

communication, health, property development, film production, vocational training, education and teaching.

Two types of businesses are not covered by the IIC. These include businesses open to foreign investment but which are also subject to authorisation. Also falling outside the IIC are businesses in the insurance, brokerage, transport and merchant services sectors which require authorisation and that also have 50 per cent-plus foreign participation. Foreign investment is free for wholly export-oriented businesses and foreign participation can be up to 100 per cent of the project's equity without prior authorisation (see Exhibit 6.6). Foreign investments in farming cultivated land, fish farming and fishing are limited to 66 per cent.

Foreign investments of up to 50 per cent can be freely made in listed and unlisted Tunisian companies. Investments above this ceiling are subject to the approval of the Higher Investment Board.

Foreign investors defined as non-resident are exempt from most exchange regulations and may transfer returns on direct or portfolio investments at any time without prior authorisation. This applies to both principal and capital in the form of dividends and interest. Under foreign currency regulations, non-resident companies must have both non-resident individuals who own at least 66 per cent of the capital and their capital financed through imported foreign currency.

The Tunisian dinar is convertible for current account transactions covering most bona fide trade and investment operations. Full convertibility of the currency is expected but no date has been set. Central bank authorisation is still needed for some foreign exchange operations.

Exhibit 6.6

Levels of foreign ownership

Category	*Capital ownership*	*Comments*
Businesses free from authorisation	100%	Manufacturing industries Tourism Fully-exporting services Industry-related services
Businesses subject to authorisation	50%-plus	Some local market-oriented services with foreign equity share exceeding 50%
Agriculture	66%	
Fishing	66%	Fish farming Fishing
Share purchases	50%	Tunisian operating companies
Capital transfer	Free	Foreign investors are free to repatriate profits and invested capital asset disposal deriving from income, in hard currency

Free trade zones

In the free trade zones (FTZs) at Bizerte and Zarzis, companies can carry out activities as residents or non-residents. Investments in hard currency or in convertible dinars in these zones are freely made and must be declared to the free zone developer. Entities established in FTZs by companies with headquarters abroad are considered to be non-residents.

Arbitration and other international agreements

An arbitration code has been drawn up by Tunisia, which is also a member of the International Centre for the Settlement of Investment Disputes and a signatory to the 1958 New York Convention on the Recognition and Enforcement of Foreign Arbitral Awards.

Tunisia has an agreement with the World Bank's Multilateral Investment Guarantee Agency (MIGA), and investment protection and double taxation relief agreements with most OECD countries. As well as bilateral and multilateral agreements to protect investments and other rights in several areas, Tunisia is a signatory of the United Nations Conference on Trade and Development (UNCTAD) agreement for licences and trademarks protection, and a member of the World Organisation for Intellectual Ownership.

Investment incentives

Several incentives are available. Some are dependent on the sector, regional location or environmental impact of the investment and some are reserved for wholly export-oriented enterprises. Common incentives are:

- tax relief on reinvested profits and income of up to 35 per cent of income or profits subject to tax;
- customs duties exemption for capital goods that have no locally-made counterparts;
- VAT limited to 10 per cent on capital goods imports (1999 Finance Act provisions); and
- an option to choose the reducing balance method of depreciation for production material and equipment with a useful life of more than seven years.

Wholly export-oriented enterprises may be eligible for the following incentives:

- full tax exemption on export-derived profits for the first 10 years and thereafter for a 50 per cent exemption for an unlimited period;
- full tax exemption on reinvested profits and income;
- duty free import of capital goods including vehicles for transporting merchandise, raw materials, semi-finished products and services needed by the business; and

- an option to sell 20 per cent of production on the local market.

Investments that promote agricultural growth may be eligible for the following:

- full tax exemption on reinvested profits and income;
- full tax exemption for the 10 first years of operation; and
- a suspension of VAT on imported capital goods that have no locally-made substitute.

Investments in fish farming and horticultural and other projects that use geothermal water may be eligible for state support in respect of infrastructure expenses amounting to the following:

- 7 per cent bonus on investment value;
- 8 per cent additional bonus on investment value for agricultural investments in hard-climate regions: Gabès, Gafsa, Médenine, Kébili, Tataouine and Tozeur; and
- 25 per cent additional bonus on investment value for fishing projects in the northern coastline ports from Bizerte to Tabarka.

Investments in environmental protection and waste processing projects may be eligible for the following:

- 50 per cent tax relief on reinvested profits and income;
- a charge on profits and income at the reduced rate of 10 per cent;
- 20 per cent bonus on investment value; and
- a suspension of VAT on most capital goods.

Education, training, cultural production, health and transport investments may be eligible for the following:

- a deduction of reinvested profits up to 50 per cent of net profits subject to corporate tax;
- reduced tax at a rate of 10 per cent on income and profits; and
- a suspension of VAT for imported capital goods when no locally-made substitute is available.

Additionally, the state will also contribute towards the cost of social security contributions for investments that recruit Tunisian university graduates. The state will also absorb part of the cost of social security contributions incurred by companies moving to 24-hour operations.

Priority and incentive zones

The economic wealth that is focused along Tunisia's Mediterranean coastal strip and major cities has bypassed some of the country's hot, arid and less hospitable interior. Consequently the investment code accords special status to investments in areas defined as either incentive

Dome, Matmata

zones or priority zones:

- full tax exemption on profits for 10 years and a 50 per cent tax base reduction for a new period of 10 years;
- full tax exemption on reinvested profits and income;
- assumption by the state of the employer's contribution to the social security legal scheme, equivalent to 15.5 per cent of the payroll, during the first five years.

Additionally, the state may contribute towards the cost of upgrading or establishing certain infrastructure.

Exhibit 6.7
Incentive zones

Region	*Locality*
Béja	North Béja, South Béja, Medjez el Bab
Gabès	Mereth
Kairouan	North Kairouan, South Kairouan
Mahdia	Sidi Alouane, Melloulech
Sfax	Menzel Chaker
Sousse	Kondar
Zaghouan	Zaghouan, El Fahs, Bir M'cherga

Exhibit 6.8
Priority zones

Region	*Locality*
Béja	Nefza, Amdoun, Testour, Teboursouk, Goubellat, Tibar
Bizerte	Djoumine, Sejnane, Ghezela
Gabès	Old Matmata, New Matmata, El Hamma, Menzel el Habib
Gafsa	All localities
Jendouba	All localities
Kairouan	El Ala, Hajeb el Ayoun, Echebika, Sbikha, Haffouz, Nasrallah, Oueslatia, Bouhajla, Cherarda
Kasserine	All localities
Kébili	All localities
El Kef	All localities
Mahdia	Ouled Chamekh, Hébira, Essouassi, Chorbane
Médenine	North Médenine, South Médenine; Sidi Makhlouf, Ben Guerdane, Béni Khedèche
Sfax	El Ghraiba, El Amra, Agareb, Djebeniana, Bir Ali ben Khélifa, Skhira, Kerkennah
Sidi Bouzid	All localities
Siliana	All localities
Sousse	Sidi el Hani
Tataouine	All localities
Tozeur	All localities
Zaghouan	Ez-Zriba, Ennadhour, Saouaf

Investments in incentive zones may be eligible for a bonus equivalent to 15 per cent of the amount invested. Incentive zones are in a number of localities, as shown in Exhibit 6.7.

Investments in priority zones may be eligible for a bonus equivalent to 25 per cent of the amount invested. Priority zones are in the localities shown in Exhibit 6.8.

Organisations

FIPA

The Foreign Investment Promotion Agency (FIPA) plays a major role as an intermediary between Tunisia and potential and existing investors. It has three main functions:

1. inform investors about market conditions and opportunities in Tunisia;
2. provide guidance for new projects; and
3. assist investors already established in Tunisia.

To inform investors about market conditions and opportunities in Tunisia, FIPA organises marketing events and tailors programmes for foreign business executives on exploratory visits in Tunisia. During these programmes executives meet with representatives of Tunisian institutions and companies according to their business and field of interest.

A team of investment experts is prepared to steer new projects, to advise and support potential investors, and to assist them with public or private bodies in Tunisia. In assisting investors already established in Tunisia, FIPA closely cooperates with ministries to deliver a customised support service for each investment.

Specific services provided by FIPA include:

- identifying competitive investment niches;

- providing information on Tunisia's website advantages;
- organising receptions and business trips;
- researching possible site locations;
- disseminating information on foreign investment; and
- disseminating data related to project implementation.

In addition to its offices in Tunisia, FIPA has representations abroad. Activities carried out by its foreign offices in Paris, Chicago, Brussels, Cologne, London and Milan include:

- organising marketing events;
- participating in specialised shows;
- liaising with corporates and small- and medium-sized businesses (SMEs);
- providing information and advice on the Tunisian investment environment;
- identifying Tunisian partners for joint-ventures; and
- organising business trips in cooperation with professional bodies.

Every year FIPA publishes a wealth of useful information about the Tunisian investment environment in several languages. As well as general information it produces sector-specific publications on the electrical, electronic, automobile components, food and the clothing and textiles sectors.

Videos and CD-ROMs provide presentations of Tunisia's economy, investment opportunities and its comparative advantages in specific sectors. FIPA also produces publications in various formats related to the legal and regulatory framework for investment. These cover the Investment Incentives Code, the Arbitration Code, foreign trade law and law related to the financial sector. FIPA also provides bespoke information on topics such as site locations, available financing tools, as well as various general and sector-specific statistics.

Chambers of commerce

Several bilateral chambers of commerce based in Tunisia work to forge, maintain and develop international partnerships with Tunisia:

- Tunisian-German Chamber of Commerce and Industry;
- Tunisian-American Chamber of Commerce;
- Tunisian-British Chamber of Commerce and Industry;
- Tunisian-French Chamber of Commerce and Industry;
- Tunisian-Italian Chamber of Commerce and Industry;
- Tunisian-Hungarian Chamber of Commerce and Industry;
- Tunisian-Dutch Chamber of Commerce and Industry.

Specialist investment agencies

Agencies working to promote and support investments in specific sectors are:

- Agency for Agricultural Investment Promotion (APIA);
- Agency for Promotion of Industry (API);
- Export Promotion Centre (CEPEX);
- Tunisian Tourism National Board (ONTT).

Other agencies useful to potential and existing investors include:

- Industrial Estate Agency (AFI);
- Tourism Estate Agency (AFT);
- Environment Protection National Agency (ANPE);
- Vocational Training Tunisian Agency (ATFP);
- Tunisian Employment Agency (ATE);
- Training of Trainers and National Engineering Centre (CENAFFIF);
- Social Security National Fund (CNSS);
- National Institute for Standardisation and Industrial Property (INNORPI);
- National Olive Oil Office (ONH).

Investment opportunities

Tunisia offers numerous investment opportunities. Many of these are within its traditional industries, particularly in areas such as textiles, clothing, agribusiness and metal manufacturing where there are clear opportunities to use existing skills, resources and sectoral support mechanisms as a base on which to develop businesses producing higher value export products. In tourism there are multiple opportunities to develop activities that focus on the top end of the market leisure and health products. New opportunities are emerging in the communications and electronics sectors and other hi-tech activities that are developing rapidly, establishing Tunisia as a world capital in the new economy.

Privatisation and the environmental vocation

Opportunities for foreign investors have long been associated with FDI and privatisations. The government's privatisation plans are discussed in Chapter 3. Joint ventures between foreign and Tunisian companies are encouraged. Opportunities exist in all areas of the established and new economies.

Since 1996, when the government announced plans for its first independent power project (IPP), there is now a new and growing set of opportunities arising for private participation in concessions. The Rades II IPP project is expected to boost the role of build-own-operate (BOO) or build-operate-transfer (BOT) schemes in power generation, waste management, transport and maritime facilities.

Two concessions currently under consideration relate to a water purification station and a waste treatment facility. The new purification plant will be built with capacity to meet the needs of around 1.4 million people living around its planned locations of El Attar area, west of Tunis (see Exhibit 6.9). The plant aims to meet future demands for water. It aims to reinforce the wastewater treatment capacity in the greater Tunis area, raise sanitation service levels, reduce coastal pollution and promote the efficient re-utilisation of processed water for agriculture. After studies are complete, the choice of the private developer will take place upon a restricted consultation of companies selected from a pre-qualification tender. Work on the project is expected to last at least two years, starting in 2001. The BOT concession will last 25 years. An investment of TD70 million is called for.

The Household Refuse Processing Project (see Exhibit 6.10) will require an investment of TD34.5 million and includes civil engineering work and the construction or supply of equipment. Civil engineering work entails the development of platforms, setting collection and discharge systems, water drainage systems and building construction work.

Exhibit 6.9
Sample project: El Attar Water Purification Plant

Investment	*2011 (deadline)*	*2016 (deadline)*	*2023 (deadline)*
Equivalent population	700,000	1,000,000	1,400,000
Water flow (m3/day)	60,000	100,000	150,000
Pollutant load (kg dbo5/day)	34,000	40,000	60,000
Mobilisation of additional resources (Mm3/year)	22	36	54
Irrigation area (hectares)	2,000	4,000	6,000
Purification rate (%)	90	95	98

Exhibit 6.10
Sample project: Household Refuse Processing Project

Location	*Waste quantity in t/year*	*Dump area in ha*	*Estimated cost of phase one*	*Status*
Kairouan	36,000	18	3	finished implementation studies
Sousse	158,800	32	7.5	–
Sfax	137,000	25	8	–
Monastir	122,800	15	7	–
Gabès	57,000	30	4	–
Medenine	18,000	10	2	–
Jerba	31,000	22	3	–

Such schemes highlight both Tunisia's determination to encourage private investment and the high priority – unusual for an Arab/African country – that it gives to environmental schemes. As any visitor to Tunisia will agree, the country's commitment to tackling pollution and maintaining a sustainable environment has created a pleasant place to visit and work – itself an intangible, but important incentive to investors. In terms of quality of life for management and workers, Tunisia rates high, giving added weight to its claims to be a pole of attraction for investment into the new Mediterranean economy.

7 *Transport, water and energy: connecting Tunisia*

Fulfilling Tunisia's trading vocation and ambitions to become a major hub in the 21st century Mediterranean communications has required significant investments in infrastructure. These projects support and stimulate the new economic and social frameworks now under construction, both reinforcing international links and fitting with President Ben Ali's determination that no region of the country should be ignored in the developmental process.

A range of major transport, communications and other infrastructure projects are under way, variously financed by the Treasury, multilateral or bilateral support mechanisms, and increasingly by private capital. The indicative projects listed in this section outline just some of the major infrastructure works either under way or planned in the diverse range of projects to connect Tunisia.

Transport priorities reflect Ben Ali's development agenda

The transport infrastructure facilitates and is sometimes the catalyst for economic development. Thus, it plays an important role in helping Tunisia achieve its economic objectives. Moreover, it supports economic activity, and directly influences distribution costs in the productive sectors. Consequently, the objectives in the government's transport strategy are driven by the need to put in place infrastructures that promote the competitiveness of Tunisia's productive sectors, reinforce the national economy and facilitate the country's integration with the rest of the world.

The government's strategy to develop and upgrade the transport sector hinges on the following priorities, which are to:

- substitute public with private capital to finance key works, particularly in investments in the ports and highways;
- transfer commercial services from the state to private operators to reduce costs and improve productivity;
- promote the integrated development and use of various modes of transport;

- position Tunisia in the international transport network so that industry obtains logistical advantages and the means to efficiently distribute goods to export markets at competitive prices;
- promote private/public partnerships in the transport sector;
- remove rules, regulations and other restraints that may constrain Tunisian operators trading in an international context;
- provide better targeted subsidies for urban transport;
- eliminate restrictions and lighten the burden of customs on imports; and
- revise the role of central administration by reassigning certain technical functions to specialist organisations.

Exhibit 7.1

Transport investments, 1997–2001 (TD million)

Railways	421
Roads	981
Ports	596
Air	1,090
Total	**3,088**

Source: Equipment and Housing Ministry.

Public investment in the transport sector has so far been closely targeted (see Exhibit 7.1). Port projects have focused on improving facilities to maintain industrial productivity and export capabilities. Investments in roads and airports projects have often been designed to facilitate the growth of tourism. Investments across all transport sectors have aimed to facilitate economic activity.

Road construction builds a new spine for the country

Tunisia has a well-distributed road network which needs improving. According to Equipment and Housing Minister Slaheddine Belaïd:

> For a decade the total number of road vehicles [in Tunisia] has increased an average of 7 per cent a year, the national total of automobiles has thus doubled, increasing to 70 cars for 1,000 inhabitants. Because of this growth in traffic, some sections of the Tunisian road network are congested: over an area of 160,000 kilometres, we have a roads network of 19,000 kilometres, two-thirds' or 12,200 kilometres, of which is asphalted. The motorway network still comprises only 140 kilometres of highway between Tunis and M'Saken - but its extension is under way.

Under the National Motorway Programme (Programme Autoroutier National), a total of 887 kilometres of new and refurbished motorway-equivalent roads will provide free-flowing arteries for Tunisia's road traffic (see Exhibit 7.2).

There will be four highways with Tunis at the hub of all of them. The existing stretch of southern highway from Tunis to M'Saken will extend first to Sfax and later to Gabès and then to the Libyan border. The western highway from Tunis will reach Bousalem before running on to the Algerian border. Two more highways will separately connect Tunis to the cities of Bizerte and Fahs.

Exhibit 7.2

National Highway Programme, progress to end-December 2000

	Length (km)	Estimated cost (US$ million)	Status
Southern Highway	600	800	
Tunis-M'Saken	140		In service
M'Saken-Sfax	97		Study completed, planned in 10th Plan (2002–06)
Sfax-Gabes	152		Detailed study concluded
Gabes-Libyan border	180		Preliminary study concluded
Western Highway	176	480	
Tunis-Medjez el Bab-Oued Zarga	67		Opening in 2004
Oued Zarga-Bousalem	55		Detailed study concluded
Bousalem-Algerian border	84		Preliminary study concluded
Tunis-Bizerte	51	150	Opening in 2002
Tunis-Fahs	60		To study
Total	**887**		

Source: Ministry of Equipment and Housing.

The Highway Development Fund (Fonds de Développement des Autoroutes), funded by a part of privatisation receipts, will help to pay for the highways programme. Private capital will also play a part. The Tunis–Bizerte highway is to be part-financed under a build-operate-transfer (BOT) concession framework, with a payback period of between 20 and 30 years.

Urban and rural infrastructure

The government has extensive plans to improve the interior road network to boost the rural agricultural economy and plans to have built 6,000 kilometres of roads by the end of 9th Plan. But the most spectacular infrastructure works are the new roads and impressive bridges now sweeping across Tunis.

Rising up on the shore of the now shiny waters of Lac Nord is the equally shiny new Berges du Lac mixed development. The reclaimed brownfield site is now flecked with greenery and accommodates several large Tunisian and international companies, commercial centres and a leisure centre. A similar project at Lac-Sud, near the port of Tunis, boasts a pleasure park and marina.

Perhaps the most breathtaking of all the city's landmarks will be the Pont La Goulette-Radès. Work on the TD96.7 million bridge, due to open in 2005, will begin in 2002.

These structures contrast starkly with the fast-growing traffic congestion in central Tunis and its new suburbs where, house builders to the new middle classes are building new estates, often in the modern Arabian architectural style – rather than in the French colonial style which was so associated with 20th century Tunis.

The capital has thus developed because of priorities articulated in the 9th Plan, according to Belaïd:

> Investments in infrastructure total TD1.2 billion over five years. We have paid particular attention to peripheral urban express ways over these last years, especially Greater Tunis. Our approach here has been to reduce traffic congestion and consequent pollution. Therefore, to avoid traversing cities, we have multiplied exchange routes, bridges, tunnels and peripheral routes that complete the radial express ways.

Other major works in the capital involve the renovation of the capital's most famous artery, the Avenue Habib Bourguiba. There, rubber plants are being meticulously removed and replanted in fresh ground, manifestly a testament to Tunisia's commitment to the environment. New shopping malls are appearing across the capital to meet the demands of Ben Ali's 'middle class society'.

Housing is not the problem experienced elsewhere in North Africa

Surprisingly to the outsider, Tunisia has 2.2 million units of accommodation and only 1.95 million households (1999). More than 80 per cent of Tunisians are homeowners (1999) and standards of accommodation are improving rapidly. With an overstock of accommodation, the government now sets qualitative targets for housing, such as reducing population density from 5.2 inhabitants per house in 1994 to 4.9 in 1999. According to Minister Belaïd:

> Each time that we announce these figures abroad, people are astonished - but they are true; it's the fruit of a policy which began at independence, when the government paid attention to family planning, education (especially of girls) and housing. This policy was considerably strengthened since the 1987 change, date of President Ben Ali's accession and the new era.

New building continues to improve the quality of the housing stock. The current programme specifies a building programme of around 50,000 new houses each year. Around 10 per cent of these will be built by public companies; property developers will erect the remainder. The government, through the state-owned housing bank, Banque de l'Habitat (BH), makes finance available on very attractive terms for house-building projects. The government is also committed to replacing or renovating old housing stock.

Railways

Tunisia's 2,268-kilometre railway network carries 13 million tonnes of goods and 35.4 million passengers per year. Two state-owned rail companies operate in Tunisia:

- Société Nationale des Chemins de Fer Tunisiens (SNCFT) operates all mainline passenger and goods services to cities and towns, the southern Tunis-Borj-Cedria suburban services and the electrified Métro du Sahel service connecting Sousse with Monastir and Mahdia.
- Société du Métro Léger de Tunis (SMLT), operates a 45-kilometre network of five lines in greater Tunis as well as the electrified 20-kilometre Tunis-La Goulette-La Marsa (TGM) line.

New building continues to improve the quality of housing stock

Institutional reforms have reshaped SNCFT's structure and redefined its role, particularly in its relations with the state. It now has responsibility for arranging finance for capital works while the state now plays a less hands-on role than it did, although it still defines the obligations that the rail company must discharge. Reorganisation has also seen SNCFT divided into business units for transporting phosphates, general freight, inter-city and suburban passenger transport (Sahel and Tunis), infrastructure and maintenance. The reforms aim to transform SNCFT into a commercial transport enterprise operating on level terms with its competitors. Therefore, it should specialise in market segments where it can viably provide customers with better services and terms of trade than other modes of transport.

Public road transport

On average, Tunisians make an estimated 65 journeys each year on public road transport. SNT (Société Nationale de Transport) provides public transport in Greater Tunis. SNTRI (Société Nationale de Transport Interurbain) and 12 regional companies respectively provide national and regional road transport services.

Privatised public road transport is currently limited to routes in greater Tunis where Société de Transport en Commun de Voyageurs (TCV) and Société de Transport Urbain de Tunis (TUT) ply nine routes with a combined fleet of 76 vehicles.

Improvements in public transport are a central plank in Tunisia's transport development strategy. Reduced fares for students account for 54 per cent of business and barely meet 10 per cent of the cost the state contributes towards service provision. This is part of an equation that eventually calculates that the state subsidises two-thirds of public transport costs. To reduce state costs, studies are under way to increase participation in public transport by the private sector operating under service level agreements.

Providing passengers with a reliable and economic public transport between Tunisia's major towns and cities is a key government objective. Private-sector taxi services are playing an increasing role in servicing cross-country public transport.

Road haulage, previously monopolised by 14 state operators, is open to the private sector. Opening this sector up to private enterprise has resulted in the establishment of 250 enterprises and 700 owner-drivers. This has forced down the costs of road haulage.

Tunisia's maritime vocation: ports and shipping

Compagnie Tunisienne de Navigation (CTN) and Société Nouvelle de Transport de Kerkennah (Sonotrak) operate passenger services. There are also six privately-owned shipping companies.

Tunisia's ports remain publicly owned, but private-sector participation is being encouraged on a concession basis for operators and on a build-operate-transfer (BOT) basis for investments. According to Transport Minister Hassine Chouk:

> In volume terms, Tunisia has sufficient port capacity but it is not divided up satisfactorily. Rades/La Goulette [in Tunis] is under pressure, and therefore needs extending. We will undertake studies soon to almost double it, probably on a BOT basis.

Mr Hassine Chouk also plans a major redevelopment in Sousse, where the port is in the town centre. In an estimated TD170 million project, it is planned to convert the existing facility into a marina complex with pleasure port, while a new commercial port will be built outside the city.

Annual maritime traffic totals around 6,000 vessels and Tunisia's ports handle 25 million tonnes of goods each year.

Air transport: new airports planned

Tunisia has seven airports with capacity for 10.45 million passengers and which service more than 67 foreign airlines.

According to Transport Minister Hassine Chouk, a new airport is planned for the tourist zone between Hammamet and Sousse, which will help meet huge demand by taking some of the flights that now go into the country's two main airports, Tunis-Carthage and Monastir. In December 2000, Chouk told the authors of this book that a study by the state airports authority, OACA, had identified a site outside Enfidha which could serve the Cap Bon/Hammamet and

Sousse/Sousse Nord regions. Studies to build this major facility – initially costed at TD447 million – have already begun.

Also planned is a second terminal at Djerba, which is now receiving 1.5 million passengers a year, and is at saturation point. A studies tender for this project – provisionally costed at TD55 million – was out as at the beginning of 2001.

Exhibit 7.3
Tunis Air: fleet composition

	2000	*2001*	*2002*	*2003*
Airbus A300	2	2	2	2
Airbus A320	11	11	12	12
Airbus A319	2	3	3	3
Boeing B 737-500	4	4	4	4
Boeing B 737-600	6	7	7	7
Boeing B 737-200	4	4	4	4

The expansion of existing airports would boost passenger capacity to 12.95 million passengers. The volume of air traffic has soared in line with Tunisia's burgeoning tourism industry.

Contrary to some expectations, state airline Tunis Air will most likely not be privatised until at least 2005 although 20 per cent of its stock is privately held since it raised TD800 million on the stock exchange.

In 2000, it acquired two Airbus 300-600s and took delivery of three Boeing 737-600s and an Airbus A320. It is committed to expanding its fleet of aircraft over the next few years (see Exhibit 7.3).

Connecting Tunisia: some indicative funded projects

Rail network modernisation

FUNDING ORGANISATION: European Investment Bank (EIB).
PURPOSE: The development of rail transport as well as the private sector.
AMOUNT: €25 million for rail network completion and modernisation, mainly in the Sousse area. €25 million (second tranche of global loan facility advanced in 1998) for medium- and long-term financing of companies in the production and services sectors, undergoing restructuring, expansion and modernisation of their activities.
DATE: May 2000.
OTHER: Rail schemes are to be implemented by Société Nationale des Chemins de Fer Tunisiens (SNCFT) over the period 2000–05.
FINANCING: Company financing loan open to whole Tunisian financial sector. Approved Tunisian intermediary banks will on-lend the EIB funds to investors in local currency. Company financing loan was open to Amen Bank, Banque de Développement Economique de la Tunisie, Banque de Tunisie, Banque International Arabe de Tunisie and Union des Banques pour le Commerce et l'Industrie. Both loans are under the new Euromed mandate.

Development of priority roads

FUNDING ORGANISATION: European Investment Bank (EIB).

AMOUNT: €53.1 million loan for financing of eight road improvement works in Greater Tunis, Beja, Fouchana-M'hamedia, Gabès and Nabeul. €30 million from risk capital resources to build equity of private companies undergoing modernisation and public companies, recently privatised or being privatised.
DATE: November 1999.
OTHER: Roadwork loan, follows loans totalling €98 million, allocated in 1994, 1995 and 1997.
FINANCING: During an initial phase, the credit line was open to the following financial intermediaries: Banque de Développement Economique de la Tunisie (BDET), Banque de Tunisie, Société de Participation et de Promotion des Investissements (SPPI), the TUNINVEST Group, COTIF sicar and SIDCO sicar.

Tunis–Bizerte motorway

FUNDING ORGANISATION: Kuwait-based Arab Fund for Economic and Social Development (AFESD).
PURPOSE: Loan and guarantee agreement to support the Société Tunisienne des Autoroutes' building of the 51-kilometre Tunis–Bizerte motorway.
AMOUNT: Loan US$77.4 million. Total highway cost is estimated at US$132 million.
DATE: May 1999.
OTHER: Completion of motorway expected mid-2002. The term of the loan, which will carry a 4.5 per cent interest rate, will be 22 years, with a five-year grace period.

Water

Water supply and disposal have been key priorities for the government for social and economic reasons. Many major projects have already been completed. Since independence in 1956 the mobilisation of 22 large dams, 100 hill dams, 500 hill lakes, 120,000 tube wells and other facilities has reduced Tunisia's exposure to irregular rainfall and recurrent drought.

Launched in 1990, the National Water Resources Development Plan aimed to provide 1.4 billion cubic metres (bcm) but has only generated 1 bcm. Irrigated areas have expanded to 345,000 hectares (ha) from 256,000 ha and drinking water is now supplied to 78 per cent of villages, compared with 33 per cent before the plan. Exhibit 7.4 shows an overview of the water sector.

By the end of the 9th Plan (1997–2001), the authorities aim to meet the potable water demands of nearly 80 per cent of rural households, 100 per cent of urban areas and all the requirements of industry and tourism.

Water's strategic importance is most pronounced in the agricultural sector, which consumes 85 per cent of water resources. Consequently spending on the water infrastructure has been very substantial, amounting to US$2 billion or 37 per cent of the public investment budget for agriculture during the 9th Plan. Only about 7 per cent of agricultural land is irrigated, but it

Exhibit 7.4
Water sector overview

Total quantity of water	5 bcm
Number of water reservoirs	22 with a 1.9 bcm capacity
The National Company for Water Distribution (SONEDE) supplied:	
Consumers (1998)	1.4 million (200,000 in 1974)
Production (1998)	326 mcm (142 mcm in 1974)

Source: SONEDE.

generates 45 per cent of agricultural output. Several major water projects have aimed to increase Tunisia's irrigated acreage.

In terms of potable water supply and sanitation, the World Bank estimates that without major projects and reforms, increasing demand would inevitably lead to water shortages by 2015. For this reason the government, supported by several major donors, has conducted a number of key studies, culminating in the comprehensive Water Sector Review (WSR).

Completed in April 1999 by the World Bank and endorsed by the government, the WSR provides a strategy for integrated water resource management in Tunisia. Consequently all future investments in the water sector will fit this strategy. Better access to safe water and improved agricultural productivity are key strategic objectives.

In addition to policy and institutional reforms, the strategy calls for investments in water infrastructure projects that improve:

- irrigation management (including small and large-scale perimeter rehabilitation);
- groundwater management;
- conservation of water resource base and environmental protection;
- rural water supply; and
- capacity-building.

Challenges across projects include finding ways to integrate the management and conservation of water and ensure that water in irrigated areas is used economically. Technical challenges included determining how to increase the interconnectivity of water supplies and improve surface and ground water management and monitoring systems using real-time data. Discovering ways to better manage and preserve water in good rainfall years is a priority.

At a later stage, projects will begin to look at ways to increase the use of non-conventional water resources through desalination or by re-using wastewater, for example.

Water project file

Water Sector Investment Project
Part of the World Bank Group's Country Assistance Strategy for Tunisia.

AMOUNT: US$101 million.
DATE: June 2000.
OTHER: The project's two main objectives are (a) to promote effective integrated water resource management and (b) promote conservation of water resources and protection of the environment. These two objectives are expected to significantly improve the productivity of agriculture and access to safe water in rural areas.

Sousse drinking water treatment plant
Technical bids for construction contract are being studied by state water company Société Nationale d'Exploitation & de Distribution de l'Eau (Sonede). Bidders include Cadagua (Spain), Biwater (UK), a German group including Wabag and Preussag Wassertechnik, and a French consortium led by EPPM. Due for completion early-2002.
SIZE: Planned for 500 litres a second.

Tunis South Lake clean-up
The 42-month process began in March 1998. Work includes installation of locks and gates. The surrounding area will be developed into recreational land and residential plots.
DEVELOPER: State-owned Société d'Etudes & de Promotion du Lac de Tunis Sud.
CONTRACTS: Van Oord ACZ Overseas (Netherlands) and Dredging International (Belgium) – US$70 million dredging and landscaping.
FINANCING: US$43.3 million EIB loan. US$7.6 million Belgian government loan. An estimated US$8 million Netherlands government grant. Remainder to be financed through Generale de Banque and ABN AMRO commercial loans.

Dams, pipelines and water channels
ORGANISATION: Kuwait-based Arab Fund for Economic and Social Development (AFESD).
PURPOSE: Construction of the El Kebir and El Mouli dams and three pipelines, and channelling water from the Wadi Kebir, Wadi Bouterfas and Wadi Zirka into the northern Tunis water system. Additional supply will be used for drinking water and industrial and tourism projects.
AMOUNT: US$92 million loan.
DATE: April 2000.

Finance for water resource projects
ORGANISATION: Kuwaiti Fund for Arab Economic Development (KFAED).
AMOUNT: Around US$26 million (KD8 million).
DATE: April 2000.
OTHER: The loan is repayable at a 3 per cent interest rate and is to be reimbursed over 20 years with a four-year grace period. Kuwait intends to reinvest the interest on its investments in Tunisia.

Pollution clean-up in the Gulf of Gabès
ORGANISATION: EIB is financing a programme to clear pollution from the Mediterranean Gulf of Gabès.
AMOUNT: €45 million.
DATE: June 1999.
OTHER: The 20-year loan with a five-year grace period is at open interest rate that will be determined at each payment with a 3 per cent bonus to be financed with EU funds.

Dam construction programme
ORGANISATION: Kuwait Fund for Arab Economic Development.
PURPOSE: To finance the building of 11 mountain dams.
AMOUNT: Unspecified.
DATE: June 1999.

Enhancement of drinking water supplies
ORGANISATION: European Investment Bank (EIB).
PURPOSE: Second loan to help fund programme to build small earth hill dams in rural areas throughout Tunisia for supplying water for households and irrigation.
AMOUNT: US$35.6 million second loan; US$95 million total.
DATE: December 1998.

Energy

Power

Ambitious targets have been set by state power utility Société Tunisienne de l'Electricité et du Gaz (STEG) to meet Tunisia's demand for power, rapidly growing at an estimated rate of 7 per cent annually. Installed power capacity in 2000 was 2.3GW, of which 48 per cent was thermal, 15.3 per cent combined cycle, 33.7 per cent gas turbine, 2.6 per hydropower and 0.4 per cent wind power sources. Exhibit 7.5 illustrates Tunisia's historic and anticipated power generating mix and the fast-pace electrification.

Investments by STEG in the electricity infrastructure in 2000 amounted to TD287 million. In 1999 investments amounted to TD195 million, allocated as follows:

- TD75 million for distribution projects;
- TD47 million for transportation projects;
- TD39 million for production projects;
- TD18 million for logistics and building works;, and
- TD16 million for gas projects.

In previous years STEG has made greater investments. In 1998 it spent TD304 million and in

Exhibit 7.5

Power production and distribution

	1962	*1987*	*1997*	*1999*	*2000*	*2001*
Installed power (MW)	116	1,405	1,967	2,384	2,384	2,855
Thermal	–	848	830	1,145	–	–
Combined cycle	–	–	364	364	–	–
Gas turbine	–	492	712	804	–	–
Hydropower	–	65	61	61	–	–
Windpower	–	–	–	10	–	–
Production (STEG)(GW)	288	4,016	7,387	8,639	9,220	9,660
Thermal	–	3,195	4,333	5,225	–	–
Combined cycle	–	–	2,080	2,186	–	–
Gas turbine	–	708	930	1,138	–	–
Hydropower	–	113	44	90		
Electricity sales (GWh)	240	3,547	6,558	7,648	8215	8,900
Number of clients (millions)	0.18	1.14	1.95	2.12	2.22	2.36
Rate of electrification (%)	21	70	92	94	95	96
Rural	–	30	79	85	89	91
Urban	98	100	100	100	100	–

Source: STEG.

1997 TD308 million. The power utility records much smaller investment totals of TD155 million and TD133 million in 1996 and 1995 respectively.

The flagship US$260 million Rades II Carthage 471MW gas turbine project signals the start of a new era in financing power infrastructure. It is Tunisia's first independent power plant.

Connecting Tunisia: indicative power projects

Rades II Carthage combined-cycle BOOT plant

Gas turbine to be operational by mid-2001 supplying 25–30 per cent of country's power needs to state utility STEG.

SIZE: 471MW. Two 120MW gas turbines and a 231MW steam turbine.

COST: US$260 million.

PRICING: US$0.01954/kWh.

DEVELOPER: Carthage Power Company a JV of PSEG (US), Sithe Energy (France/US) and Marubeni (Japan).

FINANCING: US$92.8 million commercial debt facility syndication. Arranger – Paribas and Sanwa Bank. Participating banks – Arab Bank, Barclays Capital, Crédit Lyonnais, Dexia, Dresdner Kleinwort Benson, Industrial Bank of Japan, and KBC (Belgium). US$72 million Japan Bank for International Co-operation loan with full political risk cover. €14.1 million letter of credit standby facility. Equity – US$100 million from developer.

Ambitious targets have been set to meet Tunisia's demand for power

CONTRACTS: ABB Alstom Power (France) – US$180 million engineering, procurement and construction (EPC) contract. Arabian International Construction (Egypt) – US$20 million civil works package. Fifteen companies have been short-listed for the mechanical works package and 10 for electrical installation.
OFFTAKE: STEG.

Sidi Daoud wind-power plant, Cap Bon
SIZE: 330 kW from 32 generators.
COST: Estimated at US$10 million.
DEVELOPER: MADE, subsidiary of Endesa (Spain).
OFFTAKE: STEG.

Zarzis BOO gas-fired plant
Government approval and regulatory permits still required
SIZE: Planned for 25MW.
DEVELOPER: JV of Centurion Energy (Canada), Caterpillar Power Ventures International (US) and CME International.
EQUITY: Probable – Centurion 50 per cent, Caterpillar/CME 50 per cent.
CONTRACTS: Caterpillar expected to supply electric power equipment.
FUEL SUPPLY: Gas from Centurion's El Biban field and Ezzaouia.
OFFTAKE: Power purchase agreement (PPA) to be completed with STEG.

Rural solar electrification project
Project to equip 2,500 housing units with a photovoltaic system.
FINANCING: US$0.96 million from Spain's official credit institute (30 years' maturity including 10 years grace at 1 per cent annual interest) and similar-sized export credit arranged by Spain's Bilbao Argentaria Bank (five years' maturity at 7.14 per cent annual interest).

Tunisian/Libyan power grid
225kV grid link to complete the Mediterranean grid, which already includes Egypt and Algeria. Morocco, Spain and Italy to join by mid 2001.
FINANCING: Arab Fund for Economic & Social Development and the two governments.
CONTRACTS: Estimated at US$63 million to Siemens (Germany) to build power station in Medenine (Tunisia); KEC (India) installing 600 kilometres of power lines.

Bir M'Cherga power station
General Electric to build the gas-powered station.
SIZE: 240MW.
COST: US$80 million.

Oil

Development activity at producing and non-producing fields together with prospecting, exploration as well as seismic acquisition and interpretation work is directly aimed at boosting Tunisia's declining oil production. Improved production would also have a positive impact on the country's energy balance. While power generators are increasingly turning to gas as their preferred fuel, oil is still used in Tunisia's domestic energy supply. Apart from direct revenues from crude oil sales, increased oil production would also provide feedstock for the country's downstream sector, which is set to acquire a new refinery.

As well as reducing Tunisia's import refined product requirement, additional refinery capacity coupled with increased crude production and a move to gas for power generation would provide a boost for crude and refined liquid hydrocarbon exports. A detailed discussion of Tunisia's oil industry is contained in Chapter 8.

Connecting Tunisia: indicative oil projects

Isis field
Producing since mid-2000. Further development under way. New production flows expected by end-June 2001.
OPERATOR: Coparex Netherlands.
EQUITY: Coparex 50 per cent, Atlantis Technology Services 50 per cent.
CONTRACTS: Norway's Brovig Offshore – four-year US$60 million FPSO contract. Brovig UK subsidiary – US$0.5 million pre-engineering contract. Sarost (local) – offshore support.

Sabria concession, Kebili block

Hungary's MOL has agreed to sell its 50 per cent stake in the Kebili block and its 45 per cent stake in the Sabria production-sharing agreement to Tunisian Athanoer, a local subsidiary of US-based Athanor Resources. A 12-kilometre pipeline will take Sabria oil to the El-Franig pipeline.

COST: Sale was valued at around US$15 million.

SIZE: 5,180 square kilometres.

OUTPUT: Test wells – Sabria Ouest: 1 600 b/d, Sabria Nord Ouest: 1 1,200 b/d and 70,000 cubic metres/d gas.

OPERATOR: Athanoer.

EQUITY: Kebili as a whole – Athanoer 50 per cent. PSA – Athanoer 45 per cent, ETAP 55 per cent.

El Hamra permit

2,000 kilometres seismic reprocessed. New seismic planned. Seven prospective areas for additional exploration identified. Four-year exploration concession may be sought.

SIZE: 1.1 million acres.

OPERATOR: Eurogas (Canada).

EQUITY: Eurogas 100 per cent working interest – bought First Calgary's 33.3 per cent and TransAtlantic Resources' 33.3 per cent in 1999.

Jorf exploration permit

Initial mapping identified four leads. Evaluation planned including reprocessing seismic. Results from Bazma well (BZMS-1) will determine need for further seismic.

SIZE: 1,065,000 acres.

OPERATOR: Eurogas (Canada). Acquired in late1999.

EQUITY: Eurogas – 65 per cent.

Bazma permit

Well drilled, December 1999. Seismic interpretation delineated a large prospect. Test well was initially planned for the fourth quarter of 2000.

RESERVES: Estimated up to 1.2 billion barrels and 400 million barrels recoverable.

SIZE: 499,200 acres.

OPERATOR: Eurogas.

EQUITY: Eurogas – 40 per cent, Mobil Exploration and Producing Ventures Tunisia Inc. – 40 per cent, First Calgary Petroleum – 15 per cent, Largo Petroleum – 3 per cent and Rigo Oil Company – 2 per cent. ETAP has the right to buy into 50 per cent of development.

Tabarka permit

SIZE: 4,816 square kilometres.

COST: Plans to invest TD1.5 million (US$1.3 million).

CONTRACTS: Seismic – Carthago Oil Company (local).

Fejaj onshore permit.

Plans exist to re-enter and deepen the Chott Fejaj-3 well to test a sub-salt prospect.
SIZE: 900,000 acres.
PRODUCTION COST: Potential US$1–US$2.50/b.
RESERVES: Estimated at 150 million–300 million barrels.
OPERATOR: Bligh Oil & Minerals (Australia).
EQUITY: Nuevo Energy – 37.5 per cent, Bligh – 17.5 per cent, Coho International and Antrim Energy.

Grombalia block – Al Manzah and Belli fields

Drilling completed at the Belli-1A re-entry well, testing the Abiod formation. Discoveries at the Belli-3 well and nearby in the Zinnia field. Seismic continues. Portion of Al Manzah/Belli production reliant on the future of the Tiper oil refinery. Al Manzah-2 well production under way. Al Manzah-3 location chosen and scheduled drill in December 2000. Al Manzah development plan includes restarting production at Al Manzah-1 and drilling development wells in 2001.
SIZE: Grombalia 517,712 acres.
OUTPUT: Al Manzah-1 well – reached 5,000 b/d. Al Manzah-2 – initial 9,000b/d.
RESERVES: Al Manzah - an estimated 15 million barrels proven and probable.
OPERATOR: Ecumed Grombalia (Centurion Energy International subsidiary).
EQUITY: Grombalia permit – Centurion 37.5 per cent. ETAP has a 50 per cent option.

Anaguid onshore permit, Ghadames Basin

Reprocessed seismic and new 2D during 2000. Commitment for one exploration well by end-2001. Permit located 15 kilometres from existing pipeline facility. Nuevo Energy Company bought half of Bligh Tunisia's stake in July 2000.
SIZE: 1.1 million acres.
RESERVES: Potential of 50 million–200 million barrels.
OPERATOR: Anadarko Petroleum.
EQUITY: Coho Anaguid – 45.83 per cent, Anadarko – 33.33 per cent, Bligh Oil – 10.42 per cent, Nuevo – 10.42 per cent.

Tatouine block

Seismic completed in 1999. Two wells to be drilled during 2000–04 period.
SIZE: 1.8 million acres.
OPERATOR: Petro-Canada.

Alyane Permit, Gulf of Gabès

Four-year exploration permit signed in June with two optional three-year renewal terms.
3D seismic expected early-2001 with an exploratory well in late-2001/early-2002.
SIZE: 171,000 acres.

OPERATOR: Nuevo Energy.
EQUITY: Nuevo – 100 per cent.

Mellita exploration and exploitation permit
Centurion subsidiary, Ecumed Petroleum Grombalia, acquired the permit in mid-1998. Existing seismic shows potential for large finds. Remapping, reprocessing and acquisition of new seismic under way.
SIZE: 864,500 acres.
EQUITY: Centurion subsidiary, Ecumed Petroleum Grombali – 100 per cent.

Robbana property, Djerba island
Step out well and additional development wells planned.
SIZE: 11,856 acres.
RESERVES: Booked proven reserves – 126,000 barrels. An estimated.12 million barrels potential recoverable.
OUTPUT: Cumulative production 200,000 barrels. Robbana-1 well – tested at 80 b/d net.
OPERATOR: Centurion.
EQUITY: Centurion – 80 per cent.

Jenein South licence
Jenein-1 discovery in 1998. License expires Oct 2001.
OPERATOR: Marathon.
SIZE: 1,900 square kilometres.
EQUITY: LASMO – 40 per cent and Marathon.

Jenein North Block
Drilling was due in 2000.
EQUITY: Anadarko and Agip.

Borj el Khadra licence
Reprocessing seismic. Acquisition of 500 kilometres of new 2D seismic was planned for the fourth quarter of 2000. Well will follow seismic.
OPERATOR: LASMO.
SIZE: 5,186 square kilometres.
EQUITY: LASMO – 100 per cent equity.

New seismic
Fugro-Geoteam has completed and processed 3,800 kilometres of non-exclusive 2D seismic data for ETAP. The data includes six open offshore blocks: E1-Bargou, E2-Nabeul, E3-Mahdia Offshore, E4-Kaboudia, E5-Ramla and E-6 Sidi Mansour.
CONTRACTS: FPSO – Fugro's own Geo Baltic vessel.

Open bidding round

ETAP is awaiting tenders for 20 blocks released in March. Onshore – blocks C1 to C4 in the centre of the country and S1-S5 in the south. Offshore – N1-N4, in the north and E1-E7 on the east coast. Chall (SMIP), Chorbane (Anschutz), Kelibia (Anschutz), Nord des Chotts (ETAP) and Takrouna (CMS Energy) blocks are also under negotiation.

Skhira oil refinery

COST: First phase US$125 million; total investment US$700 million.
CAPACITY: Initially 2 million tonnes a year rising to around 8 million t/yr.
OIL SUPPLY: Algeria is a potential supplier. Seventy-five per cent of initial production for local market, future expansions to provide for export.

Gas: the fuel of the future

Gas is increasingly the fuel of choice for Tunisia's power generators. A detailed discussion of the gas industry is contained in Chapter 8.

Connecting Tunisia: indicative gas projects

El Biban field

El Biban-1 well linked to company's onshore processing facility by an 18-kilometre marine pipeline. Associated gas has been flared thus far pending installation of a gas-driven power plant.
RESERVES: Estimated proven and probable – 25 billion cubic feet natural gas and 5.6 million barrels oil/liquids.
SIZE: 56,316 acres.
OUTPUT: 1,400 b/d.
OPERATOR: Centurion.
EQUITY: Centurion – 73.7 per cent.

Ezzaouia Triassic permit

Study is under way to determine potential for additional development drilling. Technical data under review to determine first new well placement. Continuous field development plan needs ETAP approval.
SIZE: 9,880 acres.
OUTPUT: 2,500 b/d oil from seven wells.
RESERVES: 3–10 trillion cubic feet natural gas; and incremental reserves of 800,000 barrels per well.
OPERATOR: Centurion.
EQUITY: Centurion – 69 per cent (looking to farm out a portion of its interest).

Miskar field, Amilcar permit

Producing since 1996. Gas processed at the Hannibal Gas Processing Plant. Expansion planned 2000–05. Offshore gas compression facilities will be tendered in 2001 and installed in 2003 with three to five development wells to be drilled by 2004.

SIZE: 325 square kilometres.

COST: Estimated at US$640 million (US$120 million expansion work).

OUTPUT: 168 million cubic ft/d gas. Expansion target of 230 million cubic ft/d from 2001. Production decline expected from 2009.

RESERVES: 700 billion–1 trillion cubic ft.

OPERATOR: BG (100 per cent equity).

OFFTAKE: Société Tunisienne de l'Electricite et du Gaz (STEG) – to take all dry gas. 230 million cubic ft/d on a long-term basis (over 65 per cent of Tunisia's domestic gas demand).

CONTRACTS: Engineering support – BG Technology.

Jurgurtha gas discovery, satellite of Miskar

Reservoir complexities and high carbon dioxide content delayed development. Possibility of pumping gas directly into a custom-built power station.

COST: US$25 million on exploration in Jurgurtha and Hasdrubal South West.

OPERATOR: BG.

Hasdrubal South West

STATUS: Plans to shoot 300 square kilometres of 3D seismic in 2001, with an appraisal well in 2002.

COST: US$25 million on exploration in Jurgurtha and Hasdrubal South West.

OPERATOR: BG.

Hasdrubal gas and condensate field, Amilcar permit

Field appraisal completed 1998. Four appraisal wells drilled. First stage development expected 2002. Project is expected on-stream 2007. Gas to be piped via Miskar field to the Hannibal gas reception plant. Major infrastructure contracts expected 2005. Will be tied into to the facilities at Miskar.

SIZE: Amilcar tract - 2,724 square kilometres.

COST: US$300 million over nine years.

OUTPUT: Hasdrubal-3 (1997) - 2.1 million cubic ft/d. Hasdrubal-4 (1998) - 4.6 million cubic ft/d plus 1,800 b/d liquids.

RESERVES: Recoverable - 260 billion cubic feet and 25m barrels condensate.

DEVELOPER: BG (operator) with ETAP.

CONTRACTS: Hasdrubal preparation, and FEED contract to be awarded by 2001.

Hannibal gas treatment plant expansion project

Work underway to prepare plant to deal with increased capacity from Miskar.

Tunisia's demand for power is growing at an estimated 7 per cent annually

OUTPUT: Capacity increase at Sfax unit to 5.5 million cubic metres/day.
OPERATOR: British Gas Tunisia.
CONTRACTS: Engineering procurement, installation and construction (EPIC) - Costain Oil, Gas & Process.

El Franig and Baguel concessions
Three wells linked by a pipeline to the La Shirka port in September 1998.
OUTPUT: Combined estimated 12 million cubic ft/d natural gas and 1,750 b/d condensate.
OPERATOR: CMS Nomeco.
EQUITY: El Franig – CMS 55 per cent and ETAP 45 per cent. Baguel – CMS 49 per cent and ETAP 51 per cent.

8 *Industry, agriculture and tourism: motors of the economy*

Industry joins the global new economy

An emphasis on new economy industries is a marked feature of Tunisia's 10th Plan, an indicative document setting out the government's goals for the economy's development in 2002–06. While Tunisia is no longer a planned economy, President Zine El Abidine Ben Ali and his officials still set considerable store in the planning process, which they argue provides a coherent framework to set targets and measure the success of projects in industry and other sectors.

Some initiatives already under way point to fresh thinking in terms of industrial development. According to Minister of Industry Moncef Ben Abdallah one priority is to create financial structures capable of delivering much-needed risk capital. He envisages a public fund and a tax regime specifically designed for this purpose. Legislative changes will also be introduced to stimulate business development and, according to the minister, these measures will promote business growth and, most importantly, create new business operations to add to Tunisia's enterprise stock.

Tourism is a robust contributor to economic growth

Striking characteristics in the policies for industry now emerging is that they systemically take account of resources and capabilities already found in the enterprise stock, intend to replace habitual local practices with international best practice, and focus on improving Tunisia's competitiveness in the global market place. Ben Abdallah explains some of the government's philosophies:

> We try to strengthen classical industries such as textiles, leather and shoes and food processing and we have been conducting strategic studies through API (industrial promotion agency

> Agence de Promotion de l'Industrie) and UTICA (employers' federation Union Tunisienne de l'Industrie du Commerce et de l'Artisanat) in each activity. We have the potential to develop 13 studies in specific areas, and these studies - based on benchmarking - will clearly show our potential.

The methodology has already been tested:

> In a textile study, we used benchmarks to examine areas such as productivity, human resources and communications. The study showed we needed to invest $3.5 million to close [the gap between actual performance and best practice] benchmarks.

President Ben Ali has also called for positive actions to introduce new technologies to Tunisia's classical industries. Extensive studies leading to sector-specific technology resources are to be undertaken as public-private partnerships in 10 sectors (yet to be defined as at the beginning of 2001). These will look at ways to integrate new technologies into old economy operations.

Incubators with resources for technology start-ups have been established by API at five universities, laying the foundations for the development of a new breed of technology company, operating either in emerging business activities or providing innovative products or services to existing operations.

A sound record of achievement

Tunisia's policies for industrial growth have to be considered very sound in the light of past achievements. Large numbers of French, Italian and German companies have based themselves in Tunisia for many years, notably in the textiles and automotive parts industries. Strategies for industrial growth and to encourage firms to focus on exports have proved successful in the context of the 9th Plan that completes its five-year course in 2001, says Ben Abdallah:

> Around 85 per cent of exports are manufactured, and the year 2000 was the sector's third year of double-digit growth – and we raised exports by 14 per cent.

Although the texture of Tunisia's industrial base has diversified over recent years, its core activities remain in textiles and clothing, electrical and electromechanical manufacturing, food processing, leather and shoes, construction materials and chemical industries. In 1999, around 18,400 out of a total 63,000 new jobs were created in the manufacturing sector in which these and some new industries have made substantial contributions to the economy. According to the minister:

Manufacturing industries represent 25 per cent of GDP. Textiles are doing well, the food industry is growing and light industry is now focused on producing high quality goods and services. As for the shoe industry, it is developing at a rate of 14 per cent a year.

The *mise à niveau* initiative

One of the central planks of government interventions has been the *mise à niveau* initiative to modernise and raise production and quality standards in firms. Launched in 1996 in response to the demands of the new European Union Association Agreement and the wider need for Tunisian industry to compete more efficiently in global markets, the programme has particularly focused on preparing companies for competition in a free trade zone with the EU and other Mediterranean countries.

Its objectives are to strategically reposition Tunisian companies and the competitiveness of Tunisian products. The programme offers companies the possibility of improving productivity, of introducing new technologies, of restructuring themselves in size, organisation and financial management and of improving employee competencies.

Financial incentives are available to companies investing under the *mise à niveau* initiative. Firms have found it relatively straightforward to access support under the initiative, which requires applicants to accept a diagnostic review of their business from an official agency before submitting a formal application.

A study concluded in August 1999 found that since the initiative started in March 1996, a total of 1,061 companies had subscribed to at least one upgrading programme and some had signed up for a second programme. Out of a total of 4,200 companies with more than 20 employees, 2,000 will have become *mise à niveau* members during the 9th Plan. The study found that the programme had a tangible effect on business performance. Participant companies recorded an average 15 per cent increase in turnover, a 6.5 per cent increase in employment and noted that exports had been boosted by 18 per cent.

Measures aimed and small- and medium-sized enterprises (SMEs) are also in train. API has adopted the Task Force Project, which consists of reorganising SMEs into coherent sectoral and regional groups.

Tunisia has also initiated programmes to enable companies to obtain ISO quality certification, accreditations that Ben Abdallah says make a big difference to companies:

> The process [of obtaining quality certification] is accelerating, and there is now awareness that it is an imperative for the development of our firms.

Communications and the technology park boom

As well as measures to stimulate growth in Tunisia's classical industries, policies for the industrial sector are set to change. According to Ben Abdallah:

> As we move from the 9th to the 10th Plan and into the 21st century, there will be a change in government intervention, from quality and export towards communications and hi-tech creativity.

Tunisia has staked its claim in the new economy by creating the impressive Parc Technologique des Communications about five minutes' drive from Tunis-Carthage airport. It reflects Tunisia's overall public-private partnership strategy for the communications sector by providing

Tunisia's telecoms network is experiencing a particularly rapid phase of growth of around 17 per cent per year

space for scientific research, educational facilities and commercial sector software producers all integrated on one site.

The first phase of the project was completed in the second part of 1999 and has attracted a clutch of leading communications companies. Early occupants at the park include Tunisia's largest software development company, Cynex Software of the United States, and the BFI group, a Tunisian operation that develops software for the financial, telecommunications and healthcare sectors worldwide. France's Alcatel, German joint venture PicoSoft and a French joint venture, Omniacom, also operate out of the park.

A high concentration of more than 300 qualified technicians and engineers makes the park a preferred location for businesses in the communications sector, particularly while space is available on very competitive terms.

The complex is Tunisia's version of the US' Research Triangle Park in South Carolina, which has proved successful in simultaneously providing learning and business facilities. To this end, the Tunisian Telecommunications Research Centre and the Graduate School of Telecommunications are located at the site. Facilities not readily available elsewhere are installed at the park, including ample power supply and up-to-date communication links.

The Parc Technologique des Communications (PTC) will eventually host a mix of large companies and small companies that are backed by publicly supported pure research facilities, necessary for innovation but whose work may not yield commercially viable propositions. Education, specifically linked to providing engineering skills related to research is an important feature of the park, which aims to provide business and social networks through which everyone can speak, work, share ideas and cooperate.

Tunisia's showcase technology park will eventually provide conference halls and teleconferencing facilities as well as shops, banks, sports facilities, a gymnasium and a swimming pool. Most importantly, it will provide a model for many more such facilities. President Ben Ali has ordered his officials to create the right conditions for one such park a year at least to be established, at locations all over the country.

Tunisia's approach to the new economy has won international plaudits. The US Department of Commerce has said that the PTC demonstrates Tunisia's commitment to developing its human resources and foreign investment in the communications sector. A French economic journal, Capital, cited the park as one reason why it considered

Tunisia to be a world-class capital in new economy.

Several international companies have been interested in bidding for Tunisia's first privately operated GSM mobile telephone licence

Tunisia's goals for the communications society

Minister of Communications Technology Ahmed Friaa is unequivocal that the telecommunications sector's importance is pivotal to Tunisia's economic competitiveness and the promotion of exports. Moreover, he says the modernisation of the basic telecoms infrastructure is key to attracting foreign investment in all fields.

Tunisia is committed to integration in the new global economy and is allocating resources to realise and harness the benefits of new communications technologies. In this context the government has stated several goals, the most important of which it says are:

- ensuring widespread access to means of communication;
- providing and securing means of communication that ensure the confidence of users;
- spreading the digital culture; and
- boosting the role of the private sector in developing communications technologies in Tunisia.

Access to communications is becoming more widespread. Tunisia's telecoms network is experiencing a particularly rapid phase of growth at around 17 per cent a year. The number of subscribers to the fixed and mobile networks has passed 1 million and by end-2001, the number of subscribers is expected to surpass 1.2 million. This would increase the ratio of telephone density from 11.5 lines to 14 lines per 100 inhabitants.

Telephones

The fixed telephone network is seen as the main platform on which access to communications can be widened. The network was digitalised ahead of schedule in June 1999 and it is anticipated that the installed 3,500 kilometres of fibre-optic cables will stretch to 6,500 kilometres before end-2001. The network is capable of integrated data transmission and is equipped with technologies capable of broadband data transfer.

The programme to expand the fibre-optic network to improve transmission quality and attract 1.4 million subscribers by 2001 is one of the major goals of the 9th Development Plan and will lead to expenditures of approximately US$300 million on equipment such as switching, fibre-optic transmission equipment and modems. State investments in the communication infrastructure in the 9th Plan are expected to total about US$1.25 billion.

The international network connects with digital undersea cables through the telecommunications station at Dkhila, which was fully digitalised in 1998. International telecoms are also enhanced by connection of the mobile digital telephone network with counterparts in 48 countries as at end-2000. This has been seen as a particularly important move because, prior to this, potential investors complained that for all Tunisia's promotion of a business-friendly environment the lack of access to their GSM services showed the limits of running globalised operations out of the country.

For now, Tunisie Télécom is the only GSM mobile operator in the country and the number of mobile users remains relatively small. National mobile telecommunications networks have been installed to provide services to 100,000 subscribers currently.

Work is under way to expand the GSM network to provide nationwide coverage and increase its capacity to 400,000 subscribers in early 2001.

Several international companies have been interested in bidding for Tunisia's first privately operated GSM mobile telephone licence. At the end of 2000, by which time the authorities had anticipated the new network would be operating, the licence still had not been awarded.

Demand for subscription to the analogue mobile telephone network (RTM) has also increased due to technical improvements and increased capacity. In the first nine months of 2000, around 4,000 new subscribers joined an existing base of just 11,000 subscribers.

Private-sector participation in the telecoms sector is growing. Projects for which Tunisie Télécom has launched international tenders have included the ATM frame relay data transmission network, digitalisation of the Arabsat land station, an Audiotex access network and the extension of the cellular phone network into the interior of the country.

The internet

Tunisia was the first Arab and African state to connect to the internet when in 1991 its academic researchers started to use the medium. Progress after that was slow, but connectivity has recently improved through a gradual expansion of bandwidth, from 3 Mbps at the end of 1997 to 15.5 Mbps in mid-2000. A statutory framework established in 1997 provided for two licensed internet service providers (ISPs) for enterprises and individuals and seven ISPs to connect educational, research and other public bodies.

ISPs for public bodies

- ATI to connect public institutions (www.ati.tn);
- IRSIT, to connect research centres (www.irsit.rnrt.tn);
- CCK (Centre de Calcul Khawarizmi), to connect universities;
- INBMI (Institut National de Bureaucratique et de Micro-informatique), to connect relevant institutions of the Ministry of Education;

- CIMSP (Centre Informatique du Ministère de la Santé Publique), to connect relevant institutions of the Ministry of Health;
- IRESA (Institut de la Recherche et de l'Enseignement Superieur Agricole), to connect relevant institutions of the Ministry of Agriculture;
- Tunisie Telecom, to connect relevant institutions of the Ministry of Communication Technology.

ISPs for the private sector

- PlaNet Tunisie (www.planet.tn);
- 3S Global Net (www.gnet.tn).

Private service providers

Tenders for private service providers to cover various parts of the country have been published. By mid-2000 the number of internet users had increased to 300,000, compared with just 111 in 1996. A new telecommunications code has been prepared and submitted to the government that will enhance access to the internet, provide more pricing flexibility in the communications sector and provide guidelines for private sector involvement in the sector.

The government has been introducing several laws to provide a regulatory framework within which electronic commerce and electronic payments can be executed securely. Recognition under the law of electronic documents and the provision of legal guarantees to secure electronic transactions preceded the launch of Tunisia's new electronic currency.

The e-Dinar

Issued through La Poste Tunisienne (post office), the e-Dinar is a virtual currency with which the public can make secure purchases of goods and services over the internet. It is part of Tunisia's strategy to create a new array of national shopping galleries.

To use the e-Dinar, the user opens a virtual account into which money can be deposited using a plastic charge card purchased at the post office. The cards carry values of TD20, TD30 or TD50, and the virtual account can be filled to these amounts. To do this, the user unveils a secret code behind a seal on each card and feeds this information to the virtual account, which is then credited to the value of the card.

Payments for goods or services are made through a secure payment gateway which acts as a secure intermediary by using encrypted messaging to send payment and collection instructions between the user, the vendor and La Poste Tunisienne. The secure payment gateway is also used by more conventional internet payment transactions, such as Mastercard and Visa and some of Tunisia's banks.

Information technology

Tunisia has a small but growing band of companies operating in the IT sector in activities such as consulting services for hardware and software installation. Software development companies

Case study: PlaNet Tunisie

PlaNet Tunisie (www.planet.tn) is one of only two commercial ISPs connecting private individuals, commercial businesses and non-public organisations in Tunisia to the internet. The country's second ISP for these user groups is 3S Global Net (www.gnet.tn). Seven ISPs connect educational, research and other public bodies.

Founded in June 1997, PlaNet first provided internet access in the following September. In several packages the company offers e-mail electronic messaging, access to the worldwide web, file transfer services, interactive discussion forums and newsgroups. It also develops and hosts web servers.

Value-added services such as modem installation and the provision of network security (firewall) solutions are also offered to the company's steadily growing customer base. A significant proportion of subscribers are corporate clients in the petroleum, telecommunications, banking and other industrial sectors.

Educating people in the use and benefits of the internet is a fundamental aspect of PlaNet's mission. It holds open days for families to surf the internet free of charge, offers initial training courses for new subscribers and stages more advanced training events for students. The company sponsors internet clubs at universities and schools and has participated in chemical, agricultural and communications fairs. Launched in May 2000 and on sale at news outlets, the PlaNet magazine preaches the benefits of the internet to potential as well as existing users.

PlaNet Tunisie's objectives have developed in parallel with market developments. The company's initial objective was to satisfy demand from companies and the general public for internet services. Now it has one department specialising in sophisticated intranet/internet solutions for businesses. Another is dedicated to developing and providing top-class services to individual subscribers.

Providing database and secure online payment architectures is a key plank in the company's strategy, particularly in the contexts of international trade and Tunisia's plans for virtual shopping galleries from which goods and services are purchased in the e-Dinar electronic currency.

Tariffs levied by Tunisia's two commercial ISPs are similar. For a basic e-mail service PlaNet and GlobalNet respectively charged TD24 and TD26 per half-year at January 2001 prices. For a professional service including e-mail, worldwide web access, file transfer and several other benefits, PlaNet charged TD120 per half-year or TD240 per year. GlobalNet charged TD120 per half-year or TD230 per year for a comparable service. Charges do not include the cost of telephone connection to the internet.

Tunisia's two commercial ISPs may face tougher competition when plans are realised to allow a limited number of new entrants into Tunisia's nascent commercial internet market.

produce integrated management software packages for hotel management, pharmacies and insurance companies as well as software for telecommunications equipment, automatic cash distributors and magnetic cards. Other companies develop multimedia software packages and some are emerging to provide website development services.

Tunisia was the first Arab and African state to connect to the internet

Domestic markets for IT companies remain small. Tunisia expected to import around 130,000 computers in 2000. Computer usage is concentrated in larger companies, financial institutions and in government services including education, health, ministries and statistics offices. Consequently, only about 5 per cent of production is exported. Despite the low level of exports, Tunisian IT firms are carving out a niche for developing high-value products, such as the local BFI group's products for the financial and healthcare markets. Most exports go to the United States, France and African countries.

IT producers are frequently partially owned by foreign companies such as Alcatel Tunisie, Hotix International, Cynex and Systel (Lucent Technologies Group). Major world computer manufacturers and software producers are however represented in Tunisia. These include Hewlett Packard, IBM, Sun, Bull, Dell, Unisys, Apple, Compaq, NEC, Sybel, Microsoft and Oracle.

Despite its small base, Tunisia expects the IT sector's competitive advantages to attract investment, particularly as it rolls out more advanced telecommunications infrastructure.

Tunisia's competitiveness is based on the availability of skills and the relatively low cost of these skills (see Exhibit 8.1).

Tunisia has around 5,000 computer experts, 200 of whom are working in computer services companies. Around 500 computer engineers or business computerisation managers graduate each year, a figure which will reach nearly 700 engineers by the year 2001.

Exhibit 8.1
The comparative costs of IT

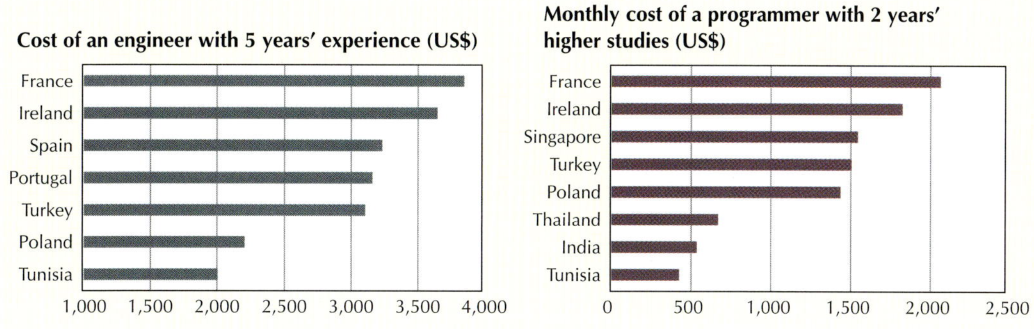

Source: Ministry of Higher Education.

Tunisia is gradually positioning itself as an attractive site for large international IT companies, some of which have recorded favourable views of the country's business environment. Germany's Siemens group established a support centre, Ettas Siemens, in Tunisia in 1990. It cites positive factors in the business environment such as the high standard of qualifications obtained by Tunisians from their studies abroad, the availability of skilled personnel at competitive costs and the flexibility and commitment of its Tunisian collaborators.

The classical economy

Since 1987 Tunisia has been steadily constructing a framework within which an increasingly diversified stock of enterprises contribute to economic growth. Tunisia's classical economy, in which the main industrial sectors are textiles, leather and footwear and food processing, now embraces more recently developed sectors and sub-sectors including electronics, automotive trades and chemicals. Industrial indices reflect robust performances from those industries most responsible for Tunisia's growth over recent years (see Exhibits 8.2 and 8.3).

The services sector has also driven the economy forward: it contributed 35 per cent to GDP and created 54 per cent of new jobs in 1999. It has developed rapidly over recent years, partly due to liberalising reforms that have attracted significant investments in some areas. The sector includes domestic trade, transport, telecommunications and financial services. Tourism has performed exceptionally well. The country's main foreign currency earner attracted TD338 million of investments, recorded 4.8 million visitors and generated revenues of TD1,954 million in 1999, double Tunisia's income from tourism in 1990.

Agriculture and agribusiness

Agriculture no longer dominates the economy: its contribution to GDP in 1999 amounted to 12 per cent. Nevertheless, farming remains crucial to Tunisia's wider economic well-being - in 1999, 22 per cent of the workforce was employed in agriculture and agricultural exports accounted for 11 per cent of aggregate national exports.

Although agricultural output in 2000 was adversely affected by drought, farm production in constant terms has grown over recent years, by 4.3 per cent during the period 1987 to 1997 (see Exhibits 8.4 and 8.5). The sector's importance is underlined by some key data:

- Agricultural exports in 1999 amounted to TD500 million;
- Total private-sector investments in agriculture and fishing reached TD680 million in 1999;
- The private sector holds 75 per cent of agricultural land;
- Government and private investments in agriculture in 1999 amounted to TD854 million, constituting 51 per cent of all investments, compared with 50 per cent in 1998 and 49 per cent in 1997;
- Tunisia is the world's leading date producer and the fourth largest producer of olive oil.

Exhibit 8.2
Industrial production index

Share of production (%)	Whole index (100)	Agri-business (15,3)	Construction materials, ceramics and glass (7,4)	Mechanical and electrical industries (9,3)	Chemical industries (6,6)	Textiles, clothing and footwear (19,5)	Other manufacturing industries (8,3)	Mines (3,6)	Energy (Hydro carbons) (23,2)	Electricity and water (6,8)
1990	100	100	100	100	100	100	100	100	100	100
1991	107,6	109,3	102,9	107,6	106,5	107,5	101,2	100,4	113,2	102,8
1992	111,8	116,7	103,0	111,1	110,7	117,7	104,1	96,0	113,3	108,4
1993	112,1	112,4	111,2	110,5	111,5	131,2	108,9	82,8	102,2	113,0
1994	117,7	118,3	113,2	118,4	125,3	146,2	115,4	89,1	96,9	119,6
1995	121,4	116,7	117,3	118,0	132,7	157,8	116,2	112,7	95,1	126,0
1996	124,7	121,6	116,4	125,0	138,9	159,2	114,1	118,7	99,6	128,8
1997	130,1	136,0	117,9	134,3	142,4	167,3	120,6	105,6	98,6	136,6
1998	138,8	136,1	127,8	153,1	152,3	180,8	131,3	128,2	102,0	144,4
1999	145,9	147,5	136,4	170,0	155,8	186,0	138,3	137,1	102,2	157,2

(Base 100 in 1990 : monthly averages).

Source: Institut National de la Statistique.

Exhibit 8.3
Industrial price index

Share of production (%)	Whole index (100)	Agri-business (31,0)	Construction materials, ceramics and glass (8,0)	Mechanical and electrical industries (11,2)	Chemical industries (5,9)	Textiles, clothing and footwear (11.3)	Other manufacturing industries (11.9)	Mines (2.2)	Energy (Hydro carbons) (12,2)	Electricity and water (6.3)
1990	100.0	100.0	100.0	100.0	100.0	100.0	100.0	100.0	100.0	100.0
1991	105.9	109.1	108.5	102.4	102.3	104.4	109.3	103.7	100.1	106.1
1992	110.1	115.7	111.8	103.6	103.7	108.2	118.2	109.1	100.0	106.2
1993	115.5	120.7	114.5	106.8	111.2	126.1	121.3	105.6	101.7	109.6
1994	119.4	125.2	113.8	108.6	116.5	131.7	131.9	97.6	101.9	114.8
1995	125.0	131.0	112.1	113.3	121.7	140.8	148.6	93.6	102.1	118.6
1996	129.6	140.4	110.4	115.8	126.9	148.7	148.6	111.5	102.1	120.0
1997	133.7	147.0	111.6	117.5	130.6	151.2	150.5	142.5	104.2	120.9
1998	137.0	151.5	113.4	120.5	134.9	142.8	157.3	157.8	109.1	123.2
1999	137.5	151.0	115.7	120.5	135.9	142.6	159.3	157.6	110.6	126.0

(Base 100 in 1990 : monthly averages).

Source: Institut National de la Statistique.

Exhibit 8.4

Agricultural production: main products except cereals (millions of tonnes)

	1988 –89	*1989 –90*	*1990 –91*	*1991 –92*	*1992 –93*	*1993 –94*	*1994 –95*	*1995 –96*	*1996 –97*	*1997 –98*	*1998 –99*	*1999 –2000*
Olive oil	54.0	130.3	165.0	285.0	135.0	210.0	70.0	60.0	310.0	90.0	180.0	195.0
Citrus fruits	259.5	236.6	226.3	185.3	281.0	208.0	194.0	210.0	211.0	229.2	210.5	225.5

	1989	*1990*	*1991*	*1992*	*1993*	*1994*	*1995*	*1996*	*1997*	*1998*	*1999*
Tomatoes	440.0	530.0	580.0	550.0	420.0	480.0	580.0	700.0	500.0	663.0	930.0
Melons & watermelons	250.0	450.0	350.0	380.0	330.0	375.0	300.0	370.0	315.0	300.0	350.0
Potatoes	180.0	217.0	220.0	218.0	200.0	210.0	233.0	270.0	289.0	295.0	320.0
Peppers	110.0	175.0	180.0	190.0	180.0	165.0	150.0	190.0	186.0	189.0	185.0
Sugar beet	229.0	289.0	210.0	290.8	245.8	231.5	270.0	305.5	268.0	142.6	89.4
Meat and offal	130.1	131.8	134.1	142.1	151.8	153.4	159.2	163.3	169.1	185.1	200.2
Milk	380.0	400.5	420.0	450.0	486.0	523.0	565.0	615.0	657.0	740.0	800.0
Fish and shellfish	95.1	88.6	87.6	88.6	83.7	87.0	83.6	84.2	89.0	90.0	93.3

Sources: Ministry of Agriculture, INS.

Exhibit 8.5

Cereal production in 1,000 quintals

	Hard wheat	*Soft wheat*	*Barley*	*Total*
1995–96	17,056	3,121	8,495	28,672
1996–97	7,232	1,617	1,690	10,539
1997–98	10,901	2,634	3,114	16,649
1998–99	11,440	2,530	4,155	18,125
1999–2000	7,100	1,350	2,450	10,900

Sources: INS, Ministry of Agriculture.

Exhibit 8.6

Tunisia agribusiness

Activity	*Number of operations*
Cereals and cereals by-products	2,750
Edible oils	1,479
Canned goods	86
Sugar	45
Vegetable & fruit packing	56
Beverages	62
Dairy products	36
Refrigeration	168
Total	**4,682**

Source: Ministry of Economic Development, 1997.

The country also produces grapes, citrus fruit, market produce and cereals. There are nearly half a million farmers in Tunisia and around 4,700 operations in agribusiness (see Exhibit 8.6). The latter are mainly small- to medium-sized firms many of which are based in or around the second city, Sfax.

The food-processing industry initially aimed to make Tunisia self-sufficient in foodstuffs but has been transformed into a thriving industrial sector. Ten years ago the country imported 70 per cent of its domestic needs for milk and milk products; now it is self-sufficient with an increasing

Tunisia is the world's leading date producer and the fourth largest producer of olive oil

export orientation. Tunisia is also self-sufficient in meat, which was in seriously short supply as recently as the 1980s.

Tunisia's competitiveness in agribusiness is attributed to the availability of competent personnel: around 30 per cent of the country's engineers work in the agricultural and agribusiness sectors. These skilled workers are trained at universities and technical institutes from where nearly 200 specialist engineers graduate every year with qualifications relevant to the agribusiness sector. There are also vocational training centres and a technical support infrastructure comprising public and private analysis and testing laboratories, research institutions and professional associations for sectoral segments such as canned foodstuffs, citrus fruits, dates, vegetables, fisheries and red meat.

Wage costs also contribute to Tunisia's competitiveness in agribusiness. The average monthly salary for an engineer with five years' experience was estimated (1998) at TD435.

EU Association Agreement

In common with other industrial enterprises, the agricultural and food-processing industries are coming to terms with the implications of closer trading ties with Europe under Tunisia's Association Agreement with the EU (AAEU). An agreement on opening up agricultural trade with Tunisia came into force on 1 January 2001. This requires Tunisia to open up its markets for cereals and oilseeds, in particular rapeseed and sunflower oil. In return, Tunisia will benefit from the EU's acceptance of an increase in duty-free imports of Tunisian olive oil from 46,000 to 56,000 tonnes for the year. This will rise by 1,500 tonnes a year until 2005.

While the AAEU already provides for the complete integration of industrial products within a huge Euro-Mediterranean free trade area, the complete integration of agricultural trade is a progressive process involving a series of bilateral agreements. The AAEU accord does not cover free entry to the European market of Tunisian products such as edible oil, citrus, fish and flowers.

Tourism emerges as a major revenue-generator

Tourism is a robust contributor to Tunisia's economic growth. In 2000, when analysts expected the revival of tourism in the Balkans and Turkey to tempt visitors away from North African destinations, the Tunisian tourism sector continued to report stronger sales, and the sector continues to grow, fuelling a hotel building boom. Tourism is Tunisia's main foreign currency earner and in 1999 attracted around TD338 million in foreign investments. Representing over 6 per cent of GDP and producing 13.9 per cent of the overall national income, the sector employs about 270,000 people. Taking into account associated jobs in crafts, transport and construction, the sector stimulates or provides direct employment to half a million people, corresponding to 20 per cent of the working population.

Some key data highlight the sector's importance:

- Foreign currency receipts from tourism rose by 7 per cent (to TD1.9 billion) in January–October 2000 compared with the same period in 1999, according to the Tourism Ministry.
- Tourist arrivals stood at 4.2 million during the first 10 months of 2000, up 5.2 per cent from the same period of 1999.
- Official estimates suggest that in 2001 the number of tourists visiting the country will top 6 million. Tunisia received only 4 million tourists in 1995.
- There are around 1,000 hotels and tourist resorts in Tunisia with a total capacity about 250,000 beds.
- Tunisia is investing US$4 billion in its tourism sector in the period to 2006.

Tunisia's main holiday products centre on the Mediterranean coast and European package tourists. German tourists stay in Tunisia most often, closely followed by French, Italian and British visitors (see Exhibits 8.7 and 8.8). Tunisia is the chosen destination each year of only 40,000 Arabs, who are less attracted by the country's marine-based holiday offering.

Tunisia has an ambitious investment programme that runs to 2006. The object of the programme is to stimulate investment in new luxury tourist resorts and diversify the products and services offered to tourists.

One market segment proving popular in Tunisia's diversification efforts is in health tourism. Several facilities built around natural spas now provide medical services on top of several other services that claim to revitalise the body and mind. Schemes under way include the new Century Tourism Project, an upmarket health and leisure venture that will include a private

Exhibit 8.7
Nationality of foreign visitors, 1995–99

	1995	*1996*	*1997*	*1998*	*1999*
French	465,103	541,878	619,891	709,023	893,664
German	837,116	808,478	858,302	883,944	1,036,262
British	239,567	206,068	248,010	263,798	261,877
Italian	245,933	270,110	314,042	328,256	354,616

Source: Office National du Tourisme Tunisien.

Exhibit 8.8
Duration of stays by foreign visitors, 1995–99 (nights '000s)

	1995	*1996*	*1997*	*1998*	*1999*
French	3,546	4,038	4,796	5,353	6,768
German	10,283	9,626	10,373	10,367	12,093
British	2,304	1,914	2,246	2,481	2,637
Italian	1,861	1,946	2,302	2,354	2,621

Source: Office National du Tourisme Tunisien.

airport, several ports, 10 rehabilitation centres and eight golf courses. Tunisia also sees itself emulating Spain and Florida by becoming an attractive destination for retirees seeking semi-permanent residence in the sun.

Textiles, clothing and footwear

They may lack the lustre of new economy industries – and there is heavy pressure from competitors in lower-pay environments, such as China, Bangladesh and Sri Lanka, as well as from closer rivals for value-added manufacturing investments (such as Hungary or Morocco) – but the textiles and clothing sectors remain among the fastest growing industries. For a decade they have maintained an annual growth rate of 10 per cent, reflecting substantial domestic and foreign investments made in spinning and weaving technologies, heavy investments in training and improvements in productivity and quality control, often the result of the sectors' involvement in the *mise à niveau* initiative. With total output in 1999 of about US$3.5 billion, the clothing and textile sectors employ around 252,000 people and a further 6,000 jobs are created every year.

The footwear sector has also recorded rapid growth. Production of shoes increased by more than 50 per cent between 1993 and 1997 and is currently increasing by around 14 per cent a year.

Notwithstanding successes to date, the clothing sector has come under increasing pressure from competitors often operating in very low-wage economies. This has led to a re-

Marina at El Kantanoui. Tunisia's main holiday products centre on the Mediterranean coast

examination of the sector and the conclusion that companies must now gain positions in world markets for higher value-added clothing. The government has installed vocational training capacity for more than 2,700 skilled workers in the clothing and textiles sectors. Trainees can acquire supervisory and managerial skills as well as technical skills at standard or advanced levels. Subsidies are available for training programmes.

Foreign investment in textiles

Much of the clothing sector's growth has been stimulated by foreign investment. Italy's Benetton is one of the most recent global companies to announce a major investment in Tunisia. It is to invest Lira20 billion to acquire a 15,000-square-metre industrial plot and establish its own manufacturing facility. The Italian clothing company will hire 3,000 workers and may expand in the future. This investment is based on a sound knowledge of the country, which is shared by the many international clothing companies which subcontract elements of their production and supply trains to Tunisian-based contractors. Around 60 Tunisian textile producers, mainly based around the industrial heartland of Sousse, counted among Benetton's suppliers, even before the new investment was launched.

Around 850 foreign or joint-venture companies operate in Tunisia, manufacturing clothing under more than 400 brand names, including Wrangler, Yves Saint-Laurent, Lacoste and Adidas.

Jeans manufacturer Lee Cooper, which established its local venture 25 years ago, is Tunisia's second largest UK investor after BG International. The company now employs 950 people and produces 3.5 million garments a year and announced in May 2000 it would invest another TD5 million modernising its Ras Jabel facility so it becomes a world-class manufacturing facility. The company said it would transfer know-how from its existing facilities through a benchmarking programme aimed at bringing the standards of its Tunisian operation up to those in its other facilities in the Far East and Europe. Its aim is to reduce production costs, improve quality standards and slash order lead times from 28 weeks to just eight weeks.

High skill levels amongst Tunisian production and supervisory staff, the country's proximity to European markets, sound infrastructure and economical labour costs are reasons given by foreign companies for investing in Tunisia. Production costs are about one-quarter of those in Italy and on a par with those in Turkey. Foreign investors also report improvements in the domestic supply chain and while in the early 1990s they used foreign suppliers, they are now subcontracting work to Tunisian companies.

Exhibit 8.9
Distribution of operations by sub-sector

Assembly of woven garments	1,188
Assembly of knitted garments	296
Knitting	127
Spinning	42
Weaving	85
Finishing	41
Other	249

Source: FIPA.

Exhibit 8.10
Distribution of operations by sub-sector

Shoe and upper producers	202
Handbags and fine leatherwork	80
Leather clothing	34
Tanneries	21
Related industries	64

Source: FIPA.

The clothing and textiles sectors are export-oriented. Of the 2,000 companies in these sectors, 1,300 produce for export only. Over 90 per cent of clothing exports are ready made, mostly woven garments (see Exhibit 8.9), and more than 80 per cent of clothing exports go to the EU. A 10-year tax holiday on profits is extended to wholly export-oriented companies, an incentive that is also available for all foreign investors. Primary textile activities are oriented to the domestic market.

Leather and footwear

The leather and footwear sector comprises more than 400 companies, about one-third of which produce entirely for export and around one-quarter of which have mixed or foreign capital. Shoes are Tunisia's fifth largest export and with improvements in quality over recent years, finished shoes are now replacing uppers as the sub-sector's main export product (see Exhibit 8.10). Italy buys around 40 per cent, France 33 per cent and Germany 14 per cent of shoe exports.

Pharmaceuticals

Tunisia's strategy for the pharmaceutical market has been to drive domestic production up. As a result, domestic production more than quintupled between 1990 and 1997, and now covers around half of the country's needs. Much of this has been achieved by major foreign companies establishing locally-based operations - many benefiting from well-qualified Tunisian staff who might otherwise have had to work abroad. Several leading foreign pharmaceutical companies are established in Tunisia. These include Hoechst Marion Roussel, Sanopi, Sandoz, Bristol Meyer Squibb, Rhône Poulenc Rorer, Beecham, Synthelabo, Msd, Upsa, Pharmacia, Upjohn, Pfizer and Jansen.

Medicines manufactured under licence represent nearly 60 per cent of production, while generic medicines account for 40 per cent. Medicine distribution is handled almost entirely by the private sector, but importation continues to be the exclusive responsibility of the Pharmacie Centrale de Tunisie (PCT). There are 1,300 retail pharmacies and 45 wholesale distributors: of which 42 are privately operated. PCT has three warehouse facilities.

Naturally for a country where medical training has always been highly valued – witness the number of qualified doctors who serve in government, and even in the upper echelons of business – Tunisia's is an expanding pharmaceutical market. It currently devotes nearly 6.3 per cent of GDP to health expenditures, considerably more than the World Health Organisation's minimum recommended spend of 5 per cent of GDP. Health expenditures are increasing at an average of 13 per cent per year, while expenditures on medicines are growing steadily at nearly 10 per cent per year.

Training for pharmacists is extensive and all pharmacists, technical agents, production heads and quality control supervisors working in existing enterprises are Tunisian. Specialists in the production and control of medicines are trained by the Monastir Faculty of Pharmacy, which each year graduates nearly 100 pharmacists. Another 2,000–3,000 higher level technicians in health are trained every year.

Investment opportunities

The most promising areas of investment in Tunisia's pharmaceutical sector are in the production of licensed or generic drugs including the areas of anti-infective or anti-inflammatory agents, cardiovascular medicines and pain-killers.

There are also opportunities in vaccine manufacture. The domestic market is estimated at nearly TD9 million, and is growing at around 16 per cent per year. This segment of activity also has considerable potential for export to neighbouring markets, particularly for veterinary vaccines. Since Tunisia imports all glass medicine packaging, there are also opportunities in the manufacture of pharmaceutical packaging.

Exhibit 8.11
Breakdown of packaging plants by activity

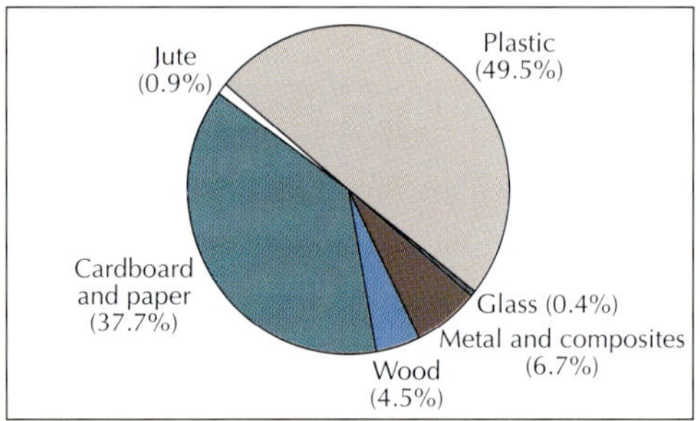

Source: FIPA.

Packaging industry booms

More than 200 packing companies produce an annual 180,000 tonnes of packaging, of which 76 per cent is paper, cardboard and plastic packaging (see Exhibit 8.11). Paper is a major industry, having grown at an annual rate of about 10 per cent over recent years and, similarly, the plastics industry has grown in recent years by an average of around 15 per cent per year.

Specific areas where there is potential for new investments in the packaging sector are in the design production of packaging for foodstuffs and in the production of bags and packaging for goods made in the textile, clothing and leather sectors.

An environmental vocation

Given Tunisia's unusually wide-ranging commitment to the environment, the packaging recycling industry is also very well developed by Arab and African standards. This involves primarily handling paper, cardboard, plastic bottles used for sterilised milk, plastic wrappings and common plastic bags.

There are particular opportunities for companies involved in recycling. Plastic waste is estimated at 64,000 tonnes per year, while recycling capacity is only 7,000 tonnes per year. Collection of used glass is inadequate: 6,000 tonnes per year are not recovered. Used metal and flexible packaging materials are not recovered for re-use. There has been progress in the collection and recycling of used paper, but further efforts are needed for the profitable use of waste paper. Consequently opportunities exist in the production from recycled materials of paper bags and labels, cardboard cartons, corrugated cardboard cartons and thin plastic film.

Because Tunisia accords major importance to the packaging sector and new recycling techniques, recycling projects are rewarded by grants of up to 20 per cent of an investment.

Tunisia is a net importer of packaging products but provides a competitive environment for producers in that it offers duty-free access to the European market, through the association agreement between Tunisia and the EU, and reasonable production costs.

Automotive components: a benchmark industry

Exhibit 8.12 shows that Tunisia is competitive as a base for industrial investments that will feed EU and other industrialised markets. It also shows that Tunisia is not an ultra-cheap labour environment; rather, investors come to Tunisia to benefit from its proximity to key markets, the high quality of its labour and a favourable investment regime. They also find it a country where the high standards maintained by leading local entrepreneurs enables them to feel secure all along the supply

Exhibit 8.12
Hourly wages in the manufacturing sector

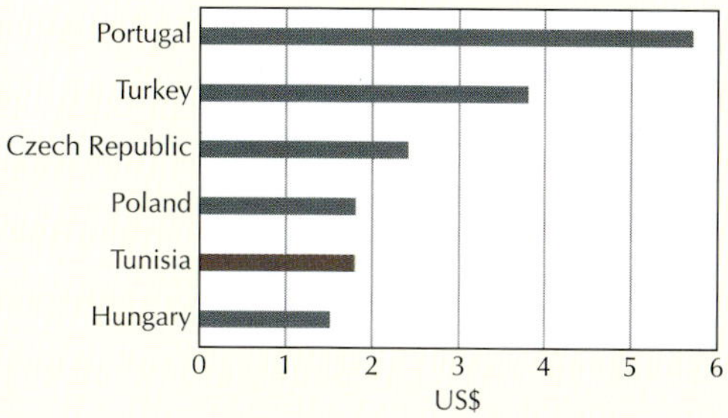

Source: Study of Specific Advantages Offered by Tunisia, KPMG London & KPMG Tunis, 1998.

chain. All these credentials are more than apparent in one of Tunisia's leading industrial success stories, the automotive parts business.

Tunisia's credentials as an automotive components supplier are well established. Peugeot buys Tunisian-made clutch parts, cable harnesses, electrical equipment and plastic parts. Some of these components are also supplied to Audi, Volkswagen, Fiat, Mercedes, General Motors, Volvo, Renault and Citroën. As well as a favourable manufacturing environment, among key factors at work in the industry are the following:

- The parts industry has built up momentum in the past decade: around 50 firms produce automotive parts from about 100 plants, most of which have ISO 9000 certification or operate in accordance with manufacturers' quality assurance charters.
- Tunisia offers a growing domestic market for spare parts - every year over 30,000 new vehicles take to the road.
- The country's strategic location offers opportunities to export to neighbouring markets.
- As vehicle manufacturers increasingly become assemblers of globally-sourced components, Tunisia is building a reputation in supplying certain components. It specialises in cable systems, exhaust systems, plastic parts such as dashboard and inner door sub-components, seat covers, rubber parts including tyres and windscreen wipers and shock absorbers.
- Tunisia is also developing the resources and capabilities to manufacture technologically advanced electrical and electronic components. These are increasingly in demand for high-specification brake, security and comfort systems.

Tunisia's competitive advantage in the automotive component sector is due to competitive production costs and skilled human resources, both at an individual level and a collective knowledge of advanced production techniques. Skills levels for the sector are maintained by Tunisia's training infrastructure. Universities are currently training 1,000 engineers per year while more than 1,000 skilled workers and technicians attend 30 vocational training centres. There are seven higher institutes of technology providing advanced training courses.

Duty free access to the European market and a rapidly expanding domestic market have attracted major foreign investors including Delphi Packard Systems, United Technologies, Draxlmaier, Pirelli and NHK Springs. Tunisia has proved a particularly attractive location for German manufacturers. Several key components produced in Tunisia would cost double in Germany. Around 47 per cent of automotive component exports go to Germany from where 41 per cent of investments in the sector in Tunisia derive. France has provided 28 per cent and Italy has provided 17.5 per cent of investments in the sector.

Mining and minerals

Tunisia has long benefited from a major phosphate industry, although in the past decade its performance has been lack lustre. To compensate for this, a recently amended mining code and Tunisia's economic and political stability have attracted several foreign miners to look to exploit other minerals in a sector that plays a significant role in the economy. The minerals sector consistently accounts for more than 10 per cent of goods exports, contributing around 10 per cent to GDP and employing about 4 per cent of the working population.

Opening up mining production to the private sector has led to clear improvements in production levels for lead and zinc (see Exhibit 8.13). Added-value in real terms in the sector is growing, by 11.7 per cent in 1999, rather slower than the 19.6 per cent growth recorded in 1998.

Mineral exports in terms of tonnage and value terms have faltered over recent years (see Exhibit 8.14), although prospects for strong export sales in 2000 are good.

Phosphates

Tunisia's mining sector is dominated by phosphate production. It is the world's fifth-largest phosphate producer. Production is largely reserved for the parastatal Compagnie des Phosphates de Gafsa (CPG), which operates 10 phosphate mines capable of producing 12 million tonnes of phosphate. Private operators are however now infiltrating the phosphates sector in a joint Tunisian-Canadian venture north of Kez.

Record output of 8.0 million tonnes was achieved in 1999, compared with 7.9 million tonnes in 1998 (see Exhibit 8.15). Promising production increases have been reported by CPG for the first half of 2000, with output of 4.0 million tonnes compared with 3.9 million tonnes in 1999.

The quality of Tunisian phosphate is poor. Most rock is extracted from Metlaoui and Gafsa. Reflecting declining world trade in phosphate rock-falling as processing operations close to mines rise, Tunisia's output is increasingly geared towards demand from local processors rather than raw state exports.

Demand for phosphate is linked to fertiliser consumption so that when prices fall, so phosphate producers are forced to take capacity out of service. World demand is expected to grow in South America, Africa and Asia but with the opening of new domestic phosphate rock mines Canada and Australia will no longer require imports.

Domestic sales account for about one-third of total sales volume and Tunisia has been successful at integrating value-added industries with mineral sector activity. The building materials, ceramics and glass industries represented around 10 per cent of industrial value-added.

Exhibit 8.13

Mineral production, 1989–99 (tonnes million)

	1989	*1990*	*1991*	*1992*	*1993*	*1994*	*1995*	*1996*	*1997*	*1998*	*1999*
Phosphates	6,610	6,259	6,353	6,335	5,476	5,655	6,302	7,151	7,222	7,951	8,006
Iron	280	291	295	332	354	288	226	239	264	222	222
Lead	2.7	3.6	1.3	1.2	0.8	3.0	11.3	7.7	2.3	7.0	10.0
Zinc	17.4	13.5	9.4	4.0	2.4	23.0	80.6	58.0	5.4	57.1	89.2
Barytes	33.0	31.0	45.0	30.0	15.0	15.7	8.1	16.0	13.0	9.0	0.5
Sea salt	528	445	406	422	375	415	319	597	437	466	455

Source: Institut National de la Statistique.

Exhibit 8.14
Mineral exports, 1995–2000

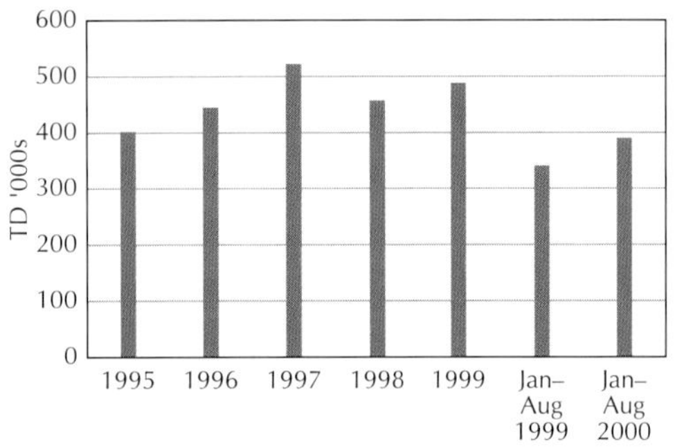

Source: Institut National de la Statistique.

Exhibit 8.15
Phosphate rock production, 1995–2000

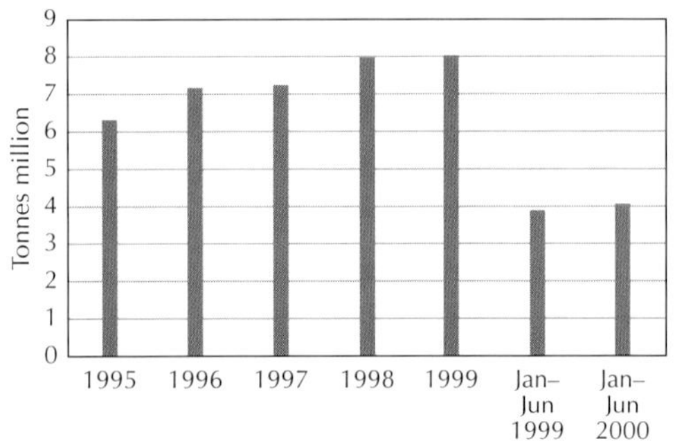

Source: Institut National de la Statistique.

In the mosaic and ceramic tiles industries, modern production techniques are superimposed over a long tradition of tile-making. Tunisia is also competitive in terms of production inputs, with labour costs around one-third of those in Italy and power available at about three-quarters of the cost of Italian energy. Tunisia's glass industry, which exports products to Europe and the United States is additionally stimulated by domestic demand from the construction industry.

Cement

In recent times, the cement sector has attracted considerable attention from investors and bankers as the privatisation of the state cement firms which long dominated Tunisian industry has unfolded. The first privatisation round concluded in 1998 when the Jebel Oust cement factory was sold to Portugal's Cimpor for US$240 million after Spain's Uniland Cementera acquired an 88 per cent stake in the US$168 million Enfidah cement company.

The final part of the second phase of the sector's privatisation programme stalled when offers received by April 2000 for Ciments Oum el-Kelil (CIOK) failed to reach government expectations.

Italian cement maker COLACEM signed a deal in May to buy Les Ciments Artificiels Tunisiens (CAT). Officials said the deal was worth TD50.5 million. CAT became the fourth out of five state-owned Tunisian cement firms to be privatised. A sixth firm, Société Ciments de Bizerte, was withdrawn from the government's privatisation programme in March 2000, soon after the successful US$250 million sale of the 660,000 tonnes per year Société des Ciments de Gabes.

Zinc and lead: Breakwater shows the way for investors

Tunisia's zinc exports more than doubled in 1999 to 74,200 tonnes worth TD17.7 million, from 31,100 tonnes worth TD7.6 million in 1998. The increase is largely due to the May 1998 resumption of production by Toronto-based Breakwater Resources at the Bougrine mine in north-west Tunisia. The mine had been closed since October 1996. Breakwater started to ship zinc concentrate in July 1998 and lead concentrate in August 1998.

Zinc and lead are found in significant quantities at Bougrine, and Breakwater Resources has been at the forefront of the government's drive to attract foreign investment to the mining industry. Breakwater was one of the first foreign mining companies to participate in the Tunisian mining sector when in 1997, through wholly-owned subsidiary, Breakwater Tunisia S.A., it acquired the Bougrine mine. Breakwater holds a 50-year concession over the ore body and it acquired, at a cost of US$19.3 million, several associated mine facilities, including a 1,200 tonne per day concentrator.

Breakwater reported mine earnings of US$8.2 million in the first nine months of 2000, compared with US$8.4 million for the same period in 1999. The company said benefits of higher zinc prices and lower site operating costs per tonne milled were offset by a lower mill head grade, lower lead prices and higher treatment charges.

Further improvements are anticipated when a new desalination plant is fully commissioned. At capacity Breakwater estimates that the zinc concentrate grade will increase to about 55 per cent and result in reduced operating costs. Breakwater is also pressing ahead with underground drilling at Bougrine. The Bougrine mine accounts for nearly all of Tunisia's zinc and lead production, the remainder coming from the Fej-Lahdoum and Boujabeur mines.

Exhibit 8.16
Crude oil and electricity production, 1989–99

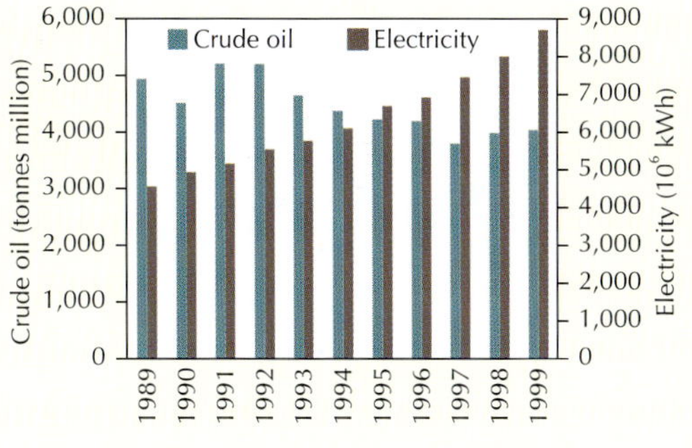

Source: Institut National de la Statistique.

Exhibit 8.17
Forecast oil production, 2001–2020

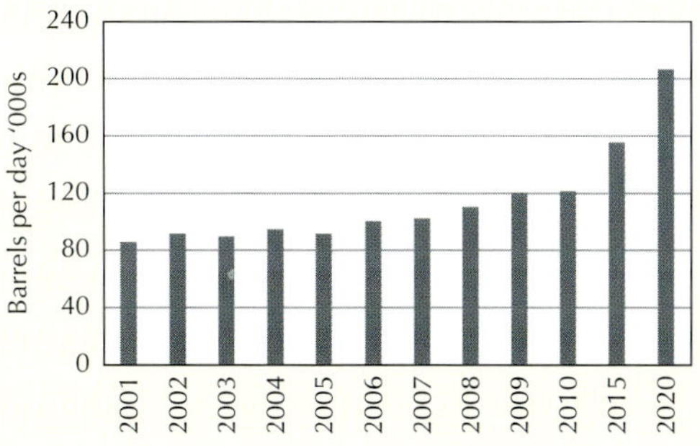

Source: US Energy Information Administration.

Exhibit 8.18
Gas production, 1991–2000

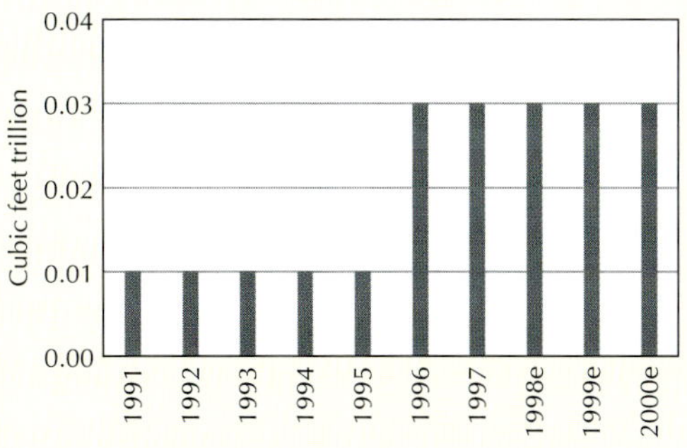

Source: US Energy Information Administration.

According to the Minister of Industry, Moncef Ben Abdallah, 10 private mining operators held prospecting licences at end-2000. One of these is Canadian junior, Consolidated Global Minerals which has an option to acquire 100 per cent interest in the Fej Lahdoum and the Djebba projects. Both projects are located in a zinc-lead prospective area, where BHP and the Metal Mining Agency of Japan have taken large land positions in the region. Billiton with Aurora, have begun exploration on the Hammalla property adjacent to the Bougrine mine while Cominco and Noranda also have interests in the region. Société du Nord-Ouest operates the lead-zinc-barite mine at Boujabeur and a zinc mine at Hassine.

The Metal Mining Agency of Japan (MMAJ) has reached an agreement with Tunisia's Office National des Mines (ONM) to explore and develop mineral resources in the north-west of the country. Under an accord signed on 18 December 2000 by MMAJ director Shinya Aoki and ONM chairman Adel Ben Hamed, MMAJ will invest up to US$3 million over a three-year period. The Japanese will explore the region located between the cities of El Krib and Mejez El Bab.

Hydrocarbons: the quest to maintain oil production

Since it peaked in the early 1990s, production of hydrocarbons in Tunisia slipped into decline (see Exhibit 8.16). Nevertheless, the hydrocarbons industry remains a major foreign currency earner and contributes around 10 per cent to Tunisia's GDP. Signs point to a turnaround and the country may soon start to realise greater economic benefits from its estimated 900 million barrels of oil equivalent reserves. A significant set of external and internally engineered factors, including new technologies, changing market conditions and reforms in the overall and sector-specific legislative and fiscal environments, are establishing a stable platform for revitalising the hydrocarbon sector.

Crude oil production fell by 9.2 per cent in the first eight months of 2000 due to declining production in Tunisia's established main oilfields, such as El Borma, Ashtart and Sidi El Kilani. Over the same period, gas production increased, resulting in a fall of 2.9 per cent in overall hydrocarbon production. Power generation, which is mainly based on the use of natural gas, grew by 7.7 per cent over this period.

Analysts had forecast steadily increasing oil production from 1997 onwards but delays due to cutbacks because of low oil prices in 1998–99 has slowed growth over the last two years. Nevertheless, forecasts for production increases based on new fields coming onstream to more than offset declining production from Tunisia's established fields are reappearing (see Exhibit 8.17).

Gas production has remained relatively level since 1996 (see Exhibit 8.18) and future increases depend not so much on gas availability but on the successful implementation of projects to recover and utilise gas. Conservative forecasts suggest demand will increase by at least 50 per cent by 2010 while others estimate demand will nearly triple by the same date.

An important factor that encourages forecasters to predict increased oil and gas production is the investment environment for hydrocarbon exploration and exploitation created by the government. The country's overall political and economic stability, enhanced by the 1999 hydrocarbon code that came into effect in 2000, has played its part in convincing dozens of domestic and international oil companies to invest in Tunisia.

Companies now find favourable operating terms, such as easier procedures and shorter deadlines relating to the granting of permits and progressive taxation. Most important are changes in gas pricing for the domestic market. Indexing the price for gas to low sulphur fuel oil in the new code is considered an equitable arrangement by investors since gas prices are now effectively pegged to crude oil prices. The previous pricing formula was considered a disincentive to investors since it linked gas prices to relatively low-priced high sulphur fuel oil. The new code also allows gas field operators to sell gas to the state electricity and gas utility Société Tunisienne de l'Eléctricité et du Gaz (STEG) and to participate in gas-to-power plants.

Speaking in October 2000, Industry Minister Moncef Ben Abdallah reckoned the new code had resulted in the number of approved prospecting licences reaching 39, representing a total investment of TD120 million.

Geological indicators and technical advances

Two fundamental but related factors underlie the government's confidence in the revitalisation of Tunisia's hydrocarbon sector: geological indicators of significant reserves and advanced technologies that make it commercially viable for the first time to find and release them.

According to ETAP geologists, the *Triassic argillo-greseux de l'interieur* (TAGI) sandstones remain one of Tunisia's most important exploration targets. Recent major discoveries have been made in the Ghadames Basin immediately to the west in Algeria, but only satellite fields have been discovered in Tunisian territory since the El Borma giant field discovery in the early 1960s.

New geological concepts and exploration techniques that have rekindled interest in Tunisia's hydrocarbons include basin modelling and seismic imaging parameters. Future oil and gas discoveries in southern Tunisia are expected by ETAP – and a growing band of oil companies – from large to medium-sized fault blocks, identified by greatly enhanced subsurface imaging with reliable data on faults and associated traps.

Anadarko of the United States believes significant tracts of its Tunisian acreage are on trend with major discoveries in its Algerian holdings. The company has a 50 per cent share of the Jenein Nord Block, contiguous with its blocks 401a and 402a operated by BHP in Algeria. Anadarko's knowledge and experience gained in the Berkine/Ghadames Basin of Algeria are being extended across the border into Tunisia, to the Anaguid permit. The 1.1 million-acre Anadarko-operated property located onshore southern Tunisia in the Ghadames Basin is on trend with the US company's prolific Hassi Berkine complex located to the west in Algeria. Under the current work commitment, the partners must drill one exploration well on the Anaguid Permit by December 2001.

Increased production over the next few years can also be expected from the prospective Gulf of Gabès, where major fields such as Ashtart, Bouri, Hasdrubal, Salambo are found. This province may contain as much as 1.5 billion barrels of recoverable oil.

Oil reserves and production

Proven oil reserves have been estimated by the US Energy Information Administration at 308 million barrels at 1 January 2000. Estimated recoverable reserves are significantly higher.

During 1999 around two dozen fields produced an average of 82,000 barrels a day (b/d) of oil, nearly all of which was crude except 1,000 b/d of natural gas liquids.

Oil consumption in Tunisia for the same year was 79,000 b/d, resulting in net oil exports of 3,000 b/d. But with crude oil distillation capacity of only 34,000 b/d and domestic demand that has increased by about 5 per cent per year for a decade, significant quantities of refined product must be imported.

Around 70 per cent of Tunisia's crude oil flows from Tunisia's old-established major but declining producing fields, El Borma, Ashtart and Sidi El Kilani. The remainder comes from around 20 smaller fields.

Some fields are managing production increases, although these are predominantly smaller permits. Production from the single-well Didon field in the Zarat permit has exceeded expectations by producing around 7,000 b/d in the first half of 2000, around twice the recorded production rate in the same period in 1999. ETAP failed to exercise an option, which lapsed in 1999, to back into the Didon development project where Tunisia's MP Zarat and Soco International of the United Kingdom have interests. According to Soco, a commitment well has been scheduled but if successful it would likely not be put on production until the Didon well declined to its economic limit. At such time, the floating production, storage and offloading (FPSO) facility that now serves Didon would be moved to serve the discovery.

Enhancement of existing fields through advanced engineering and technologies that provide better understanding of resources will extend the life of existing fields. But net increases in production will probably come from new discoveries or previously commercially unviable fields where today's technologies make development and production feasible.

Centurion Energy is an increasingly high profile producer since new production came onstream at its Al Manzah property at a rate of 4,000 b/d, adding to production at a rate of 3,550 b/d from existing fields, El Biban, Ezzaouia and Robbana (see case study).

Exploration

Private Tunisian companies are among the three dozen or more holders of prospecting or exploration permits. These include Carthago, which holds the Medjerda and Tabarka permits. The Bouchamaoui family's HBS holds licences for the Les Oasis et Nord and Médenine permits. ORI holds the Ras Marmour licence close to Zarzis and SMIP holds the Chaâl concession close to Sfax. Athanoer recently acquired a 50 per cent stake in the Kebili Block and a 45 per cent stake in the Sabria production-sharing agreement from Hungary's Mol Tunisia Oil & Gas in a sale valued at around US$15 million.

In the Gulf of Gabès, Houston-based Nuevo Energy has a 100 per cent interest in the 171,000-acre Alyane exploration permit. The concession lies directly within the prolific nummulite limestone trend where many of Tunisia's and Libya's largest fields have been discovered. The company plans an aggressive exploration campaign and will acquire 3-D seismic data in early 2001 with the aim of drilling its first exploratory well in late 2001 or early 2002. Nuevo has also acquired a 10.42 per cent interest in the Anadarko operated Anaguid Permit. Centurion's Mellita exploration permit is in the Gulf of Gabès (see case study).

Tunisia is the world's fifth largest phosphate producer

One of the most significant exploration projects in the region is the joint Tunisian-Libyan venture exploring the 7 November field, which straddles both Tunisian and Libyan territorial waters. It lies between Libya's giant Bouri field and Tunisia's Isis and Miskar fields. Drilling started in August 1999 on the block, which has estimated minimum recoverable reserves of 300 million barrels.

The 3,000 square-kilometre block is the property of the Joint Oil Company (JOC), a venture owned 50:50 by the Libyan and Tunisian governments. It will take 35 per cent –39 per cent of any profits from 7 November on which Saudi Arabia's Nimir Petroleum is operator with a 45 per cent interest. Malaysia's state oil company has a 35 per cent share and Tunisia's Medex has a 20 per cent stake.

Data availability on Tunisia's offshore geology is improving. Fugro Geoteam AS completed in 2000 the acquisition and processing of the 3,800 line kilometres seismic survey to the east of Tunisia entitled Offshore Tunisia Pelagian Shelf Survey. This provides a regionally consistent dataset across a group of open blocks with ties to a total of 40 wells of which 18 are in unlicensed areas and 21 are in licensed areas. This includes ties to the oil fields of the Gulf of Hammamet in the north and to the oil and gas fields of the Gulf of Gabès in the south.

Several companies are actively exploring in southern Tunisia the location of the giant El Borma field and where Anadarko hopes to discover fields on trend with its huge discoveries in neighbouring Algeria. Other companies with exploration interests in the region include Union Texas Petroleum and Phillips Petroleum.

Centurion is actively pursuing or considering several exploration and development projects on its five Tunisian properties (see case study).

Downstream potential for investors

The 34,000 b/d Société Tunisienne des Industries du Raffinage (STIR) refinery at Bizerte, produces insufficient product to meet domestic requirements and has long been slated for expansion.

International petroleum distributors, including TotalFinaElf, Shell, Mobil and Esso, are making inroads in a market still dominated by state-owned Société Nationale de Distribution du Pétrole (SNDP). Officials have indicated that the government's privatisation programme will include a yet-to-be defined stake in SNDP.

For the last decade, domestic demand for petroleum products has increased by about 5 per cent a year. The government's policy of subsidising fuel prices burdens the economy. By August of 2000, the absorption of higher oil prices had cost Tunisia TD103 million, although 28 per cent of this was recouped by moderate petrol price rises earlier in the year.

Gas: the growth industry

Gas is gaining weight in Tunisia's energy balance. Estimated consumption in 1998 was 104 billion cubic feet (bcf) and production was 67 bcf, leaving Tunisia to import 37 bcf. However, with reserves of 2,750 bcf, Tunisia has enough gas to meet fast-growing domestic demand for power generation, to release oil for export and for other purposes.

Two operations produce the bulk of Tunisia's gas. Associated gas from the El Borma field supplemented by gas offtaken as a transit fee from the TransMed pipeline that runs from Algeria through Tunisia to Italy provides about one-third of domestic demand.

The remaining gas for domestic demand is produced from the offshore Miskar field operated by British Gas Tunisia Limited (BGTL).

BG is the biggest investor

BGTL is a wholly-owned subsidiary of BG International, which is now Tunisia's largest industrial investor. Located in the prospective Gulf of Gabès, the 325 square-kilometre Miskar field was discovered in 1974 and contains the largest gas pool ever discovered in Tunisia with reserves of about 1 trillion cubic feet. At the end of 1999 reserves were still greater than 700 bcf but by 2009 production is expected to slow down. By this time, a second BG field, Hasdrubal should be onstream. The field is being expanded in several phases as part of BG's multi-million dollar nine-year investment programme that began in 2000.

Miskar, where sustained production began in 1996, has been supplying 168 million cubic feet (mcf) per day to the state utility company Société Tunisienne de l'Eléctricité et du Gaz (STEG), and from 2001 – after further development of the field – will increase the supply to over 200 mcf per day. Under an agreement with STEG, BG will be able to supply over 230 mcf per day on a long-term basis. BG holds a 100 per cent interest in Miskar and has already invested around US$600 million in field development, the construction of the Hannibal plant, located 22 kilometres south of Sfax, the Miskar-Hannibal pipeline and processing facilities.

The Tunisian government decided to delay production from BG's Hasdrubal gas and condensate field until 2007. Located on the Amilcar exploration permit - jointly held with state petroleum company Entreprise Tunisienne d'Activités Pétrolières (ETAP) – Hasdrubal has recoverable sales volumes of approximately 260 bcf of gas and 25 million barrels of condensate. BG may invest up to US$400 million in Hasdrubal if suitable fiscal and pricing arrangements can be made. An appraisal well will be drilled in 2002 to assess the reserves potential adjoining the discovery, after which a development plan will be finalised.

BG's second exploration permit, Ulysse, is jointly owned with ETAP. BG has also looked at the Jugurtha field, 20 kilometres west of and similar to Miskar in that it is a complex and costly to develop reservoir with high carbon dioxide deposits.

Already the largest investor in the Tunisian energy sector, BG signed several agreements in 2000 with the government, STEG and ETAP committing an additional US$450 million of investments. BG is now positioned to supply a substantial segment of Tunisia's gas needs to 2020.

Further investments in Tunisia are dependent on talks with the government, which continue up to the very highest levels. BG International's chief executive met with President Ben Ali at least twice during 2000. BG has consistently expressed its interest in more opportunities that would utilise its gas chain expertise, but these must coincide with acceptable levels of pricing - which are always the subject of tough negotiations with the Tunisian authorities. These could include, in collaboration with STEG and ETAP, gas-to-power projects and the development of compressed natural gas as a vehicle fuel in Tunisia.

CMS and other gas-based plays

The Michigan-based CMS Energy is another major international company which has taken a stake in natural gas production; CMS operates the 115-kilometre, 45-mcf/d natural gas pipeline that since 1998 has brought previously captive natural gas to market in Tunisia. Owned jointly with ETAP, the pipeline system brings gas and condensates from three wells in southern Tunisia's El Franig and Baguel concessions, in which CMS Nomeco is operator with 55 per cent and 49 per cent respective working interests. The remaining interests in the concessions, where total production is around 11.5 mcf/d of natural gas and 1,435 b/d of condensate are owned by ETAP. Gas from the wells in southern Tunisia is sold to STEG while liquid hydrocarbons are sold on world markets.

CMS is also the operator and currently holds 100 per cent working interest in the Tarfa wells in the Baguel concession, although ETAP has an option to acquire an ownership interest up to 51 per cent in any development programme. Production from these wells would also be fed into the El Franig-Baguel pipeline processing system.

Among other ventures, a consortium comprising Caterpillar Power Ventures and CME International of the United States and Canada's Centurion Energy is planning the gas-to-power project that would use associated gas currently flared in the El Biban Electric Power Project (see case study).

Tunisia has proved particularly attractive to Centurion and a few other Canadian juniors. Another of these, Eurogas Corporation, has been seeking potential partners to prospect for potentially huge gas reserves it believes are trapped in the highly prospective Triassic-age TAGI sandstone fairway that crosses the Algerian border into Tunisia and onto Eurogas' acreage. The Calgary-based junior says its initial investigations revealed that areas in its Tunisian permits contain the same type of highly prospective TAGI sandstones in which large discoveries have been made in Algeria. Eurogas holds interests varying from 65 per cent to 100 per cent in 2.7 million acres covered by three permits on the fairway.

At the same time as it announced much improved financial performance for the first nine months of 2000, Eurogas reported that discussions were under way with potential partners to drill a well during the first quarter of 2001 to test the Bazma prospect. It also said modelling of 258 kilometres of newly acquired seismic data on its wholly-owned El Hamra permit had been completed. Reprocessing has begun on 400 kilometres of seismic data on its 65 per cent-owned Jorf permit with the objective of mapping potential drilling targets. Eurogas has also negotiated extensions to its Bazma exploration and its El Hamra seismic permits. Eurogas' activities in Tunisia are still speculative, counterbalanced by production elsewhere. Companies are now looking for their Tunisian fields to be brought to production to confirm their faith that, as well as an attractive operating environment, Tunisia's geology is still capable of producing economically viable fields for oil companies of all sizes.

Case study: Centurion Energy builds up from scratch

Five-year old Centurion Energy is growing fast into a role as one of Tunisia's leading hydrocarbon producers. By the end of 2000, gross production from concessions in which the Canadian-based firm holds working interests was equivalent to around 10 per cent of national production. It has attracted the interest of some very influential backers, and has signed up for significant tracts of prospective acreage.

Centurion owns and operates over 1.4 million gross acres over five concessions in Tunisia through three wholly-owned subsidiaries – Ecumed Petroleum Tunisia, Ltd., Ecumed Petroleum Zarzis, Ltd. and Ecumed Petroleum Grombalia, Ltd. The gross unrisked potential recoverable reserves from the five Tunisian concessions are estimated at 975 million barrels of oil equivalent. The Company also holds extensive seismic coverage over its Tunisian onshore and offshore holdings.

Centurion's Tunisian interests

	Working interest (%)	*Gross acreage*	*Net acreage*
Grombalia	75	517,712	388,284
Mellita	100	864,500	864,500
Ezzaouia	69	9,880	6,817
El Biban	74	56,316	41,673
Robbana	80	11,856	9,485

Centurion's Al Manzah field on the Cap Bon peninsular, south-east of Tunis, began sustained production in October 2000 at a rate of 4,000 b/d. Production is expected to increase over the next few years. Earlier in the year the well was completed and tested at gross rates of between 1,500 b/d and 9,000 b/d. Development plans for the field, assuming the successful testing initiated in December 2000 of Al Manzah #3, could result in a total of five wells. The Al Manzah field is located on the Grombalia concession where the company says its evaluation work has identified several further leads. Plans for 2001 include conducting a 100-kilometre seismic programme to help confirm further exploration prospects and drilling at least one exploration well.

When it came onstream, Al Manzah boosted Centurion's existing Tunisian production at El Biban, Ezzaouia and Robbana. These three fields produced a gross total of 3,550 b/d gross and 1,700 b/d net to Centurion in the third quarter of 2000.

As well as its pure exploration plays, Centurion has plans to add value to its existing properties. Located 18 kilometres offshore and 30 kilometres south-east of Djerba Island in the Gulf of Gabès, El Biban is tied into the company's onshore processing facility by marine pipeline. Associated gas from the oil production has so far been flared but could be captured, sold and used if plans materialise for a gas-to-power generating plant that would market electricity to the national power grid.

Centurion is a consortium member, along with US companies, Caterpillar Power Ventures and CME International planning the El Biban Electric Power Project (SEEB). Sales of energy from the project to the national power grid are scheduled to begin in early 2002 if negotiations with potential lenders that were at a very advanced stage for the project financing of SEEB are successful.

Of several high potential exploration targets in Centurion's Tunisian portfolio, a very large and deep Triassic gas prospect on the Ezzaouia block may prove the most exciting. The prospect has estimated recoverable reserves in the range of 1-3 tcf of gas, from reservoirs similar to those encountered in prolific wells from Libya to Algeria. The company believes its net asset value would multiply significantly if it successfully realises the prospect's potential.

A study has been initiated on the Ezzaouia block and a field optimisation committee has been established comprising members from Maretap (JV operating company) and an independent reservoir engineering company. This group is assessing existing structures and reservoirs in the field in addition to other potential hydrocarbon-bearing zones. Several parties have expressed an interest in this and a second Triassic prospect on the El Biban concession according to Centurion.

The offshore Mellita permit in the shallow waters of the Gulf of Gabès commits Centurion to reprocessing 1,000 kilometres of existing seismic data, acquiring 400 kilometres of new seismic data and drilling one exploratory well. The four-year permit from September 1998 may be followed by two supplementary phases of 30 months each. Centurion is expected to seek a partner to participate in further exploration activities after data acquisition is completed. Two major oil and gas fields are located close to the northern boundary of the concession.

The one-well and about 80-b/d Robanna field holds considerable reserve and production upside according to Centurion, which seems prepared to postpone developing this property while it focuses on larger projects elsewhere in Tunisia and in Egypt.

9 *Conclusion: fulfilling a Mediterranean vocation*

Tunisia has come a long way since independence in 1956, weathering a number of political and economic storms to create a country with real potential for playing a full part in the globalised economy. President Ben Ali's genuine enthusiasm for information technology and the industries of the new century is fast making Tunisia's economy one that is able to function in the e-age. His officials are convinced that by dint of hard work and the benefits of ordered liberalisation, Tunisia can aspire to European levels of economic and social performance – as are enjoyed by smaller southern European economies such as Portugal and Greece – within the next decade.

Increasingly, economic analysts in Europe agree with this view. Indeed, Tunisia's Euro-enthusiasm and its conviction that it can compete in the single market helps to explain why no other southern Mediterranean country has proved so committed to the European Union's Euro-Med partnership initiative. Five years after Tunisia first signed this agreement, becoming the first country to do so, the affects of the Euro-Med partnership experience are now visible across Tunisia. Some Tunisian companies will disappear as levels of competition from Europe increase, but many more will succeed in the *mise à niveau* programme, to help bring them up to the European level, and this will contribute to building a much stronger economy.

This trend will accelerate during the next decade, suggesting that Tunisia will be able to attract sufficient foreign investment. FDI is already coming in at levels which have helped to make Tunisia the only North African economy yet to achieved sustained growth – which, it is sometimes forgotten, is the goal of the other countries in the region, as well as of the World Bank and IMF – and investment-grade credit ratings.

Responding to a stable polity

No North African capital is as well ordered as Tunis – a tribute not only to the attention to detail in managing populations so typical of Ben Ali's Tunisia, but also to the country's genuine commitment to development within a sustainable environment. Tunisia's urban development will continue to endow the economy with a settled, relatively well-educated population with a real commitment to maintaining a stable polity.

Improving living standards

Counter-balancing criticism of the Tunisian political system are some impressive social and economic data. President Ben Ali is presiding over an economy that routinely delivers 5–6 per cent annual growth, where foreign investment flows are rising, where the population growth rate has fallen to 1.1 per cent and housing standards are high by regional standards. Although there are wealthy Tunisians, the gaping divisions of wealth so apparent – and divisive – elsewhere in North Africa are not nearly as marked in Tunisia.

Many Tunisians hope this situation remains; while an opening to private investment in education and health is welcomed by some, many Tunisians are concerned that traditions of public services, which have served them well in the past, could be at risk in a more liberalised (and by implication divisive) economy. One of Ben Ali's strengths has been to listen carefully to such sentiments.

Tunisians are reaping the benefits of these positive trends; most of their North African neighbours have not enjoyed such improved living standards and other economic/social indicators. Where pockets of real poverty and social depravation exist – especially in potentially rebellious areas such as the south-east and big city housing projects – Ben Ali's initiatives to remove these blights (known as 'zones d'ombre') are producing real results. In tackling these ills, he is backed by a majority of the population.

As the data published in Chapter 2 suggest, Tunisia has succeeded in a remarkable social experiment, to promote women's rights as the key to building social stability and a basis for economic growth. More resources can be channelled into education and other services, aspirations can be much higher and sustained growth is achievable when the economy is not struggling to keep up with the birth rate. In contemporary Tunisia, this is no longer an equation; in neighbouring countries it is.

Indeed, such has been the extent of Tunisia's success in breaking the cycle between poverty and the birth rate, as described by ONFP director Professor Nabiha Gueddana, that Tunisian middle-class families may now contemplate having more children – and being able to comfortably educate them for the future.

Challenges for the next decade

Much remains to be done, however. Tunisia's strong economic performance has been rooted in prudent and balanced macroeconomic management that aims for continued fiscal consolidation and control over inflation, backed by a sound record of investment in social and physical infrastructure. This has delivered such prizes as Tunisia's much-vaunted investment-grade rating, which yields such dividends when Tunis goes to the markets for financing.

There have been efforts to speed up the slow pace of its microeconomic reform programme – reflected in the sale in 2000 of the country's biggest cement plants. Further large sales are expected, as is the headline-grabbing liberalisation of Tunisian telecoms. These moves will

Tunisia has come a long way since independence in 1956 and has created a country with real potential for playing a full part in the globalised economy

underline the fact that by 2001–02, Tunisia really has come a long way in dismantling the state's domination of the economy. They will encourage investment in other sectors, further entrenching the private sector's emergence as a vital force in Tunisian life.

As the decade progresses and Tunisia integrates further into the Euro-Mediterranean space, this private-sector emergence will make for a more vibrant, competitive economy. Tunisia has a real chance of making its strategy of investment-led growth, developed in the late 1980s and early 1990s, work in the 2001–12 period.

Tunisia has always had a vocation to act as a hub of trade and other business – and, at times, as a powerhouse of ideas – in the Mediterranean basin economy. The going is not always easy, but Tunisia is showing many of the signs of economic and social life necessary to show that, in future, it can meet its vocation.

The co-publishers

Foreign Investment Promotion Agency

63 rue de Syrie
1002 Tunis Belvedere
Tunisia
Tel: (216) 1 792 144
Fax: (216) 1 782 971
Email: fipa.tunisia@mci.gov.tn
Website: www.investintunisia.com

Office National du Tourisme Tunisien

1 avenue Mohamed V
1000 Tunis
Tel: (216) 1 341 077
Fax: (216) 1 350 997
Email: info@tourismtunisia.com
Website: www.tourismtunisia.com

Centre de Promotion des Exportations

28 rue Gandhi
1001 Tunis
Tunisia
Tel: (216) 1 350 344/801 698
Fax: (216) 1 353 683/333 696
Email: cepex.dg@cepex.org.tn
Website: www.cepex.nat.tn

Tunisair

boulevard 7 Novembre
2035 Tunis Carthage
Tunisia
Tel: (216) 1 700 100
Fax: (216) 1 700 008
Email: mail@tunisair.com.tn
www.tunisair.com.tn

Societe Tunisienne de Banque

rue Hedi Nouira
1001 Tunis
Tunisia
Tel: (216) 1 340 477
Fax: (216) 1 340 009
Email: stb@stb.com.tn
Website: www.stb.com.tn

Banque Nationale Agricole

rue Hedi Nouira
1001 Tunis
Tunisia
Tel: (216) 1 831 000/200
Fax: (216) 1 830 117
Email: bna@bna.com.tn

Banque de l'Habitat

21 avenue Kheireddina Pacha
B.P. 242
1002 Tunis
Tunisia
Tel: (216) 1 785 277
Fax: (216) 1 784 417
Email: banquehabitat@bh.fin.tn
Website: www.bh.com.tn

Tunisie Telecom

rue Asdrubal (en face du Centre Galaxie 2000)
Tunis
Tunisia
Tel: (216) 1 801 011
Fax: (216) 1 800 777
Website: www.tunisietelecom.tn

Compagnie Tunisienne de Navigation

5 avenue dag HammarskJoeld
Tunis 1001
Tunisia
Tel: (216) 1 341 777
Fax: (216) 1 345 736/350 976
Email: coutunav@ctn.com.tn

Groupe Chimique Tunisien

7 rue du Royaume d'Arabie Saoudite
1002 Tunis
Tunisia
Tel: (216) 1 784 488
Fax: (216) 1 783 495
Email: gct@gct.com.tn
Website: www.gct.com.tn

COMETE ENGINEERING

COMPANY PROFILE

Founded in 1987 by a number of professionals under the leadership of Mr Radhi Meddeb and with the financial participation of Tractebel Engineering (Belgium), the International Finance Corporation (World Bank Group, Washington, DC) and the Tunisian Kuwaiti Development Bank, COMETE Engineering became within few years one of the leading Tunisian consulting and engineering firms in terms of both turnover and number of staff, and especially in terms of the quality and diversity of its consultants.

Besides its traditional main areas of expertise, which include construction and infrastructure engineering on one side and strategic studies in the fields of economics and finance on the other, COMETE developed specific expertise. In this context, COMETE gained experience and know-how in supervision and management of important infrastructure projects, advice on development strategies and institutional reforms, agricultural development and environmental preservation, assistance in privatising and restructuring public firms, and advice to industrial and service firms.

COMETE through its subsidiary COMETE International derives one-quarter to one-third of its turnover either directly from public agencies in African developing countries, or through missions awarded by important multilateral funding agencies with which COMETE is registered: the World Bank, the African Development Bank, the Islamic Development Bank, the European Investment Bank, etc. The reputation and experience of COMETE lead to its frequent selection as consultants alongside well-known European and North American consulting firms.

MAJOR PROJECTS

Agricultural development

• AGRICULTURAL PERSPECTIVES FOR THE YEAR 2010. Ministry of Agriculture (Tunisia, 1995–96). A strategic study of the agricultural sector, its perspectives taking into consideration the sector's potentials and constraints, and the part it will play in the economic and social development of Tunisia by the year 2010

• AGRICULTURAL INVESTMENT STRATEGY IN ALGERIA. World Bank (Algeria, 1995–98). As part of the Structural Adjustment Plan, the study evaluated resource allocations, and defined a public agricultural investment strategy for the period of transition and, for the hydraulics sector, a specific water allocation and cost recovery strategy.

• REINFORCEMENT OF AGRICULTURAL SUPPORT SERVICES. Ministry of Agriculture (Tunisia) and World Bank (1998–2000). The mission established the requirements for the development of support services, privatisation and/or transfer to professional organisations, and finally identification of a project to be financed by the World Bank over the period 2002–2006.

Trade and direct foreign investment

• PROSPECTIVE STUDY ON THE IMPACTS OF THE ESTABLISHMENT OF A FREE TRADE ZONE

BETWEEN TUNISIA AND THE EUROPEAN UNION. Ministry of National Economy (Tunisia, 1993–94). Evaluation of the impacts of the free trade zone, proposals for a strategy, timetable and action plan for implementation, and definition of a competitive restructuring programme for the Tunisian economy.

• SPECIFIC ADVANTAGES OF TUNISIA IN THE SECTORS OF INFORMATION TECHNOLOGY AND PHARMACOLOGY. Foreign Investment Promotion Agency (Tunisia, 1997). Identification of opportunities for attracting foreign direct investments.

• COMMERCE DEVELOPMENT STRATEGY IN TUNISIA. Ministry of Commerce and World Bank (Tunisia, 1999–2000). Definition of preferential development axes and regulatory reforms; adaptation of public and private institutions to the requirements of globalisation.

• PRIVATISATION OF THE ENFIDHA CEMENT PLANT. Uniland (Barcelona, Spain, 1999). Assistance, with Paribas, in the preparation of a proposal by Uniland to acquire a cement plant in Tunisia (due diligence). The contract was awarded to Uniland for US$150 million.

• TUNISIAN SERVICES EXPORT DEVELOPMENT STRATEGY. Ministry of Commerce and UNDP (1998–99). Sector and national strategies with action plans to penetrate privileged target markets.

Important infrastructure projects

• LES JARDINS DE CARTHAGE. Private developer (1995–2000). Design and construction management of a high-quality tourist and residential complex (a 110,000 m^2 complex on a 22-hectare site).

• CONSTRUCTION OF 48 SCHOOLS IN CAMEROON. (1994–2000). Design and construction management.

• HYDRO-AGRICULTURAL INFRASTRUCTURE IN NAMENTANGA (Burkina Faso, 1998–2001). Engineering design and construction supervision.

• 7 NOVEMBER SPORTS CITY IN RADES. 2001 Mediterranean Games Organising Committee (1997–2001). Design and construction supervision of the technical aspects of a football stadium (60,000 spectators); engineering design and construction supervision of the athletics stadium and of the Olympic village.

• ELECTRIFICATION OF GRANDE COMORE ISLAND. Islamic Development Bank (Federal Islamic Republic of the Comoros, 1999–2002).

COMETE ENGINEERING
Immeuble COMETE
Avenue Hédi Karray 1082
Tunis – Tunisia
P.O. Box : 97 – 1002 Tunis – Tunisia
Phone: 00 216 1 707 800 – 00 216 1 707 900
Telefax: 00 216 1 707 200
E-mail: dg@comete.co.tn
Website: www.comete.com.tn

CORPORATE STRATEGY

Over the last 15 years, Tunisia made the wise and irreversible choice of fostering competition and openness of its economy. COMETE has followed this process by its distinguished contribution to many strategic studies, wide-ranging privatisation and important foreign direct investments in Tunisia.

COMETE intends to continue to be a privileged partner in the internationalisation of the Tunisian economy by helping local firms in their export endeavours and international firms in their positioning in the Tunisian market.

The competence of our teams, their wide range of activities and our strong ethics are guarantees for the success of our clients.

FINANCIERE TUNISIENNE

2 bis, Rue du Reservoir, 1008 Tunis, Tunisia
Tel: +216 1 562 155, 562 054, 565 195 Fax: +216 1 564 135
hedi.djilani@financiere.com.tn
Chairman and CEO: Mr Hedi Djilani
Managing Director: Mr Abdelkader Essghaïer

The group was founded in Tunisia in 1941 and has existed continuously since then in a variety of different corporate and legal forms. Since 1994 the group has held a significant stake in Lee Cooper International (London) and it holds a stake in Hygiene & Santé, which represent Procter & Gamble in Tunisia.

Financière Tunisienne group companies (affiliates and subsidiaries) include:

TEXTILES AND CLOTHING

- MTEI – created in 1959, MTEI is the pioneer of Tunisian textile manufacturing.
- CRJ – manufactures Lee Cooper-branded garments for the local market. The company is also a subcontractor of many other international brands.
- MAT – focused exclusively on the manufacture of industrial garments and clothing.
- Artois Confection – a company at the heart of the Tunisian ready-to-wear sector.

FINANCE AND INVESTMENT

- InvesTrust – an affiliate of Financière Tunisienne which focuses on corporate finance advisory and restructuring work. It is particularly specialised in business administration and financial engineering. InvesTrust advises companies on their strategic financial goals, their financing options and the optimum way to grow and deliver value to shareholders. InvesTrust has also developed a venture capital arm.
- Hannibal Lease – one of Tunisia's fastest growing commercial leasing companies active across many sectors of the economy.
- FININVEST SICAF – an investment fund focusing on both listed and unlisted equities.

TOURISM

- Karthago Group – the company owns hotels in Hammamet and Sidi Bou Said. A major refurbishment of the Sidi Bou Said property will be completed in 2001. To capitalise on the strong European market the company has created a charter airline, Karthago Airlines.
- Easy Tour – one of Tunisia's leading tour operators.

RETAILING

- Bonprix – a leading chain of supermarkets in Tunisia. The company is implementing an ambitious expansion plan in North Africa.
- BATAM Morocco – a chain of retail outlets selling household durables. It is the first Tunisian retail chain in Morocco.
- MediaStore – Tunisia's leading chain of electronics stores specialising in computers, telecommunications, audio-visual and music equipment.
- Gallerie des Marques – an exclusive chain of clothing outlets for luxury brands including: Hugo Boss, Naf Naf, Chevignon and La Perla.

TECHNOLOGY SECTOR

- LPI – the local partner of JD Edwards. LPI is a technology advisory firm for companies and institutions.
- @Home – a leading Tunisian educational software company exporting to the European market.
- INTEGER – a technology adviser that has an active web and internet development team and is expanding internationally.
- Builtech – assembler of computers for the local market.

Mr Hedi Djilani is chairman and CEO of Financière Tunisienne, one of Tunisia's premier export-oriented corporations. Besides his commercial interests Mr Djilani is a board member of the Banque Centrale de Tunisie, President of the Tunisian Federation of Private Employers (UTICA), a member of the Tunisian Parliament and a member of the Central Committee of the RCD. Mr Djilani's international interests include the presidency of the Pan-African Employers Confederation and the presidency of the International Organisation of Employers from 1997 to 1999. He has received many awards and decorations for distinguished public service including Commander of the Order of the Republic of Italy, the French *Légion d'Honneur*, as well as being appointed a *Grand Officier* of the Republic of Tunisia and a *Grand Officier* and *Grand Cordon* of the Tunisia Order of 7th November. Mr Djilani is married and has five children.

Mr Hedi Djilani

Groupe Carte

CARTE INSURANCE
Compagnie d'Assurances et de Réassurances Tuniso-Européenne (CARTE), S.A.
12, Av Habib Thameur, Tunis. T: +216 1 355022 F: +216 1 340 875 E: dgen@carte.com.tn
Chairman & CEO: Mr Hassine DOGHRI. Managing Director: Mr Abdelrahman FATMI.
Founded in 1976, CARTE, with its principal partner Le Mans International Holding, and in association with the Tunisian financial group UTP, is primarily involved in the insurance and reinsurance of the Tunisian corporate sector. CARTE is listed on the Tunis Stock Exchange and is the first Tunisian insurance company to be certified to ISO 9002 standard.

CARTE is present in all sectors of the Tunisian economy including hydrocarbons, energy, aviation, construction, manufacturing, finance and transportation. CARTE operates a highly sophisticated risk management system to ensure the correct and profitable running of its business and to assure its clients of an international standard of service.

From its solid base CARTE is constantly looking to develop and expand through prudent investments. This is illustrated by the extensive network of subsidiaries and shareholdings developed by CARTE. Some of these are shown below.

COFIB CAPITAL FINANCES (CCF): brokerage and financial advisory firm
51, Av Jugurtha, Tunis. T: +216 1 840 253 F: +216 1 843 778 E: cofcapfin@planet.tn
Chairman of the Board: Mr Hassine DOGHRI. Managing Director: Mr Slaheddine LADJIMI.
CCF is the result of the 1998 merger of COFIB (part of CARTE) and CAPITAL (a leading independent brokerage firm). CCF specialises in primary and secondary equity markets; asset management; corporate finance and advisory work; and financial engineering.

CCF has an active asset management operation comprising COFITE-SICAF and SICAV SECURITY and provides a dynamic and professional asset management service for institutions and high net worth individuals. CCF also provides stockbroking and market operations on TSE (settlement, fulfilment and registration); institutional fund management; venture capital and corporate finance; IPOs and other market offerings; and privatisation and other public-private structured finance.

CCF will launch two new SICAV funds: one for listed equities and the other a fixed income fund. CCF will open two new offices in Tunisia: one in Sfax and the other in Sousse.

COFITE-SICAF. Compagnie Financière Tuniso-Européenne
12, Av Habib Thameur, Tunis. T: +216 1 355 022 F: 216 1 340 875
Chairman & CEO: Mr Hassine DOGHRI.
Activities include the finance of the tourism sector and asset management.

COTIF-SICAR. Comp. Tunisienne d'Investissement et de Financement des Entreprises

51, Av Jugurtha, Tunis. T: +216 1 844 243 F: 216 1 845 583. E: cotif.sicar@gnet.tn

Chairman & CEO: Mr Hassine DOGHRI. Managing Director: Mr Abdeladhim ENNAIFER.

COTIF SICAR is the venture capital and private equity subsidiary of Groupe Carte. Its mission is to encourage development of entrepreneurialism, excellence and innovation by investing capital in selected start-ups, projects, growth companies. COTIF-SICAR provides entrepreneurs not only with capital but also with management, technological and marketing support.

TEMA CONSULTING. La Tuniso-Européenne de Management, S.A.

51, Ave Jugurtha Tunis. T: +216 1 844 677 F: +216 1 845 583

E: tema.consult@planet.tn Website: www.tema-consulting.com

Chairman of the Board: Mr Slaheddine LADJIMI. Managing Director: Mr Abdeladhim ENNAIFER.

Tema Consulting is a strategic management consulting firm. It is engaged in assisting companies in improving their performance metrics and in defining and realising their corporate goals. Tema's core competencies are in corporate strategy; production, logistical and quality management; financial engineering and structuring; marketing, communication and CRM; human resources; and information technology and systems.

Tema Consulting works closely with a network of market-leading partners including Groupe SOGES (Italy); Institut National Polytechnique de Toulouse (France); Formation PME Liège (Belgium); Exa International (France); and Vision Consulting (Saudi Arabia).

CITE. La Compagnie Immobilière Tuniso-Européenne S.A.

Lotissement EL Khalij, Les Berges du Lac, Tunis. T: +216 1 861 538 F:+216 1 862 193

Chairman of the Board: Mr Hassine DOGHRI. Managing Director: Mr Mahmoud BOUROUIS.

CITE is the property development arm of Groupe Carte; its main projects are:

Résidence les chatelets - Hammamet, Résidence En Naser M'nihla - Gouvernorat de l'Ariana and Résidence 'Les reflets du Lac' in Tunis on the edge of the lake.

SIDHET. Societe Immobilière et d'Hotellerie en Tunisie S.A.

Lotissement EL Khalij, Les Berges du Lac, Tunis. T: + 216 1 862 902 F: + 216 1 862 193

Chairman of the Board: Mr Hassine DOGHRI. Managing Director: Mr Ali MAAJOUL.

SIDHET has begun work on the construction of a four-star hotel complex with a 550-bed capacity and a complex of villas with private pools and gardens on a 7-hectare sea-front site.

CIIM. Compagnie Immobilière Industrielle Modulaire SA.

Lotissement EL Khalij, Les Berges du Lac, Tunis. T: + 216 1 862 902 F:+216 1 862 193

Chairman of the Board: Mr Hassine DOGHRI. Managing Director: Mr Skander LAZRAG.

CIIM is an industrial property development company. It specialises in developing, building, managing and selling industrial and economic developmental zones.